Leave It All On The Field

Leave It All On The Field

Lessons from the Athletic Field to

Life's Battlefield

Jon Stiansen

Leave It All On The Field

Copyright © 2022 by Jon Stiansen

First Printing, 2022

ISBN 979-8-412-75510-6

Ordering Information:

Available from Allonthefield.com, Amazon.com, and other retail outlets

Cover design by Brett McFarland

Dedicated to those who push me to be my best:

Jaime, Isaiah, Eli and Liv

And to my parents who modeled to me a life of faith and service.

Love you and thank you.

Contents

Preface

To start I want to tell you a little about myself. I am not a professional athlete or a coach of some championship team. I have never won the Super Bowl or World Cup or national championship of any kind. I am also not a theologian. I am a husband to my wife for the past 20 plus years and father to my three kids. I work a full-time job and then some to put food on the table and keep a roof over my family's head. I am a son and a brother. I strive to be a good friend and neighbor. I go to a local church and volunteer at my children's schools and in my community. I also have coached youth sports for the past 10 years. It was during my time of coaching that God dropped the idea of this book into my heart and has been prodding me over the years to write it.

As a child I loved sports. I loved playing hard and pushing my body. I played everything I could that my parents allowed. I was competitive by nature and wanted to be the best at whatever sport I was playing. I played baseball, soccer, basketball, football and track competitively at different times throughout my youth. As I got further into high school I specialized in soccer and track as I thought I had the best chance of getting a scholarship to college with those sports. It turns out I wasn't really a stand out in those sports either, but I knew I had the work ethic and ability to compete at the collegiate level. I became a walk-on at a college in New York after a weekend tryout for their soccer team. I also had some decent times in track from high school, and the school offered me partial scholarships in both soccer and track.

So as you can tell this book is not about my illustrious athletic career and accomplishments. This book is not a how-to book on coaching or a guide to be a better athlete, but it may be helpful in those endeavors. This book is a journey looking back at the lessons we learned as athletes and teammates on those fields and courts as we competed and were coached to be the best players we could be. This book is about taking those lessons we learned as athletes on those fields and looking at how they apply to us today to become the best we can be for ourselves, our families and our communities. In this book I am in many ways preaching to myself and asking some tough questions to the man in the mirror as I reconnect with what I learned as an athlete and as a coach. This book was written specifically for Christian men, but it is my hope that it will be beneficial for anyone reading it.

A lot of books, workbooks, seminars, and workshops are designed to help men be better husbands, fathers, leaders, workers and friends. I have read some and attended some as well, and they have been very beneficial in my life. I am not saying that I have any answers that haven't been offered before but maybe a perspective that will help you connect in a new way. I work as a psychotherapist and have seen firsthand the issues that arise personally, relationally, professionally and societally from men who neglect themselves or avoid their responsibilities and their families. Our schools, homes, workplaces, churches and prisons are a testament to that. Even with all that we know and have read, there are still so many fatherless homes and absent dads and divorces and unhappy marriages. Most of us now don't even watch the news, because it's too depressing.

What are we missing?

What message is not reaching those who need it?

This book was written as a response to a word God gave me about some of those pieces that might be missing. And in writing this there may have been answers to those issues and lessons we learned as boys and young men on the athletic fields that we have forgotten. Memories and experiences that have shaped us that we no longer apply to our daily lives today as men. I want to uncover and revive some of those lessons and examine how we can put them into practice today, so that we can have the life God has designed for us and be a help and example to those around us.

Some of you had good dads and good childhoods, and some had quite the opposite. Some of you never had a father in the home modeling to you what it meant to be a provider and protector. Some of you never even met your dad. And some of you are somewhere in between, but many of you had a coach who believed in you and pushed you to be your best.

God wants to be that coach in our lives today if we allow Him to. I pray you find this book helps you to connect with that part of you and your story and will be encouraging and uplifting in your quest to be the man God has designed and equipped you to be in order to change your world and the world around you. I also hope that if you are reading this book and don't believe in God that you find these concepts helpful to your everyday life and families as well.

We are called to love, serve and lead our families and communities. It takes a lot of determination and self-sacrifice in order to do the job right. I am not saying I have it all figured out, but there are some things I've learned along the way that I hope will help you in your journey. I've also come to realize that in my natural abilities and resources I can only go so far in my quest to fulfill those duties.

Life can often times feel like a battle.

It at times beats you up and spits you out.

It is my sincere hope that in the end you can look back at your life with no regrets.

That you gave it all you had.

That you played as hard as you could.

That you left it all on the field.

PART 1
(WHERE)

Chapter 1

<u>Where Is Your Commitment?</u>

"I don't think as a participant in life you cannot be committed. You either commit to mediocrity or commit to greatness."

-Les Brown

It's 5:30am on a Monday morning in upstate New York. It's cold, and it's dark. I stand around my teammates silently and anxiously looking at a field which has orange cones set up in its four corners lit up by the headlights of a few cars. I can see my breath in the reflection of those lights. I wonder what's in store for practice this morning. "Why are we out here so early today?" I ask myself in my head. The coach yells at us to line up behind a cone. He explains that we are going to be sprinting from cone to cone on his whistle. We won't be stopping until he tells us to stop. Most of my teammates are cloaked in shadow as we line up, and it begins. The whistle blows, and my sore and tired muscles summon the strength to go again. We run from cone to cone again and again and again. There is no break as we sprint. We do this for the next hour. It feels like forever, but no one says a word. We just keep going. Eventually as the sun begins to come up over the trees surrounding the practice field, our coach blows the final whistle, and it's done. We all stand with our hands on our knees, our lungs and our legs screaming at us. Coach tells us to hit the showers, get to class, and he'll see us back on the field at 3:00 that afternoon to go again. And you guessed it, that afternoon we run again.

Two days earlier we had our only loss of the regular season to the team that would eventually become the NAIA National Champions in collegiate soccer that year. We obviously didn't know that at the time since it was a regular season game, but we had a chance to win that game and we ran out of gas. All of our preparation and training up to that point wasn't enough. The coach knew it, and we knew it. It was now time to dig deeper and push further than we knew we could go. Our coach made us a promise that no team would ever outrun or outlast us again, and he was going to take us to that level. We would go on that season to win our league and our region and go to the national championship tournament. At that tournament we made it as far as the quarterfinals.

I know many of you who are reading this can go back in your mind's eye and recall a story or event or team you were on where your coach pushed you to that next level. It was up to you to answer that call or not. Not answering that challenge could have meant a losing season or a missed opportunity or possibly being cut from the team. Answering that call meant reaching the potential you didn't know you were capable of at the time.

There's a story in the Old Testament of the Bible that some of you may be aware of about a man named Job. God allowed trials in his life to test his level of commitment. I think that is an important distinction we need to make in our lives and our relationship with God. We often get stuck in our walk with God and angry at Him because of the trials in our lives, and we miss the purpose for the trial (James 1:2-4). We, or maybe it's just me, think "Why are you doing this to me? Things would be fine if only… (you fill in the blank of what thing you would like taken away or added to your life so that you would feel no struggle)." God is allowing the struggle, so that you can grow stronger.

When you read through the first chapter of the book of Job, specifically verses 6 through 12, you will see a conversation taking place between God and Satan. The way I read it God is asking Satan to consider his servant Job and the exemplary life he has lived. Satan responds (and I'm paraphrasing), "Of course he looks good and has it all together. You give him everything he wants and don't let any struggles come into his life. I bet if you mess with his stuff he'll curse You to Your face." Job was a wealthy man by the standard of that day, and after this exchange God allowed Satan to test Job (Job 1:12). Keep in mind Job has no knowledge of this conversation between God and Satan, and therefore has no idea he is being tested.

Satan begins to test Job, and he loses everything: his wealth, his children, his health, and his wife and friends have turned on him. His friends also accuse him of doing something wrong which he hasn't done. Throughout this time Job maintains his integrity, his faith and his commitment.

It says in Job 2:9-10 (New King James Version):

Then his wife said to him, "Do you still hold fast to your integrity? Curse God and die!"

But he said to her, "You speak as one of the foolish women speaks. Shall we indeed accept good from God, and shall we not accept adversity?" In all this Job did not sin with his lips.

Even though Job remains faithful, that doesn't mean he didn't have feelings of despair, and it doesn't mean he didn't have times where he questioned God. In fact on numerous occasions throughout the book Job cries out to God to answer for what is happening to him, and God stays quiet. It isn't until Chapter 38 that God replies:

Then the Lord answered Job out of the whirlwind, and said:

"Who is this who darkens my counsel

By words without knowledge?

Now prepare yourself like a man;

I will question you, and you shall answer Me (Job 38:1-3).

Job is angry with God, however God is going to examine Job and see where his commitment lies in life. Is he only "all good" when everything is going his way?

Throughout this book, Leave It All On The Field, the sections and chapters are a series of questions I asked myself as I wrote it, and hopefully you will ask yourself as well as you read it. I hope it will help us to "prepare yourself like a man" as we examine ourselves. God goes on through the rest of the book of Job to challenge him but let him know that in spite of what Job sees or experiences or feels; God is still in control. God has his back, and He can be trusted.

We are all committed to something in our life, if we want to admit it or not. Some are committed to their jobs or their spouse or their kids or their stuff. None of those things in and of themselves are wrong, but God wants us to be committed to Him first and foremost. He wants us to love Him with all of our heart, all of our soul, and all of our strength (Deuteronomy 6:5). It seems pretty clear where God wants our commitment to be. He wants that commitment, because that is His commitment to us. That is how much God loves us (John 3:16).

It is similar to my college soccer coach who wanted the best for us as a team. He knew to get the best out of us we were going to have some trials to get there. Imagine after our only loss of the season he got us together and said calmly "You know guys it's okay. It was a tough game last weekend. You ran out of steam out there, but that happens. You had a chance to win and you let it go, but you can't win them all. We'll just keep trying and hope for the best."

At first, as a team, we would feel a sense of relief, because the coach wasn't mad. Pretty soon though you would realize that this isn't a very good coach. Why are we out here playing every day if we aren't trying to win? Why isn't he upset with us? Why isn't he pushing us? He knows we didn't play our best. And that's it right there. You are committed to the coach, because he knows how to take you further than you know how to on your own. His job is to make you the best player and team you can be.

It is the same in your relationship with God. God, like a coach, wants to develop us into the best we can be. He allowed testing in Job's life, and He does the same in your life and in mine. It is not to punish us or because He doesn't like us. He does it to get us focused, so we can *play* at the next level.

To win in athletics takes total commitment. On the athletic field we were 100% committed. Every ounce of our being was committed. We didn't want to let our coach or our teammates down. We weren't foolish enough to think back then that we didn't need to practice. In fact you practiced for many more hours than you actually played in the game. If you wanted to excel, you practiced and played on your own. You put in hours and hours of preparation and training. Your life was committed to being the best player you could be.

Chapter 2

<u>Where Is Your Focus?</u>

"What you stay focused on will grow."

-Roy T. Bennett

So looking at the title of this second chapter you may be asking yourself what is the difference between asking myself "Where is my commitment?" and "Where is my focus?" Good question.

Commitment is a decision, and our focus determines our action.

Let me explain. If you are married then presumably you had a ceremony with family and friends and your spouse and bridal party, etc. or at the courthouse, and you made a commitment to that person. You made a decision before the state, God and loved ones that you would be with this person and no one else. If making that decision was all you needed to do in order to have a successful marriage, then I'm pretty sure the state of our marriages would be a lot better off than they are.

Let's look at another example from the world of athletics. Go into your imagination or memory bank and think about one of the teams you root for or played on where a player or teammate made a commitment to your team and turned out to be a total bust. I don't want to name any names, but we all know examples from any number of professional athletic teams where you were really excited for the upcoming season because so and so signed with your team. They made a commitment to the team. They signed the contract, and that was as good as it got. They had no focus on the field or the court. They didn't work hard. They weren't a good teammate. They had talent which allowed them to get signed but had no focus which made them fall way short of their potential.

The same goes for us. I can make a commitment to my wife or my kids or my friends or my job, but my word means nothing if I am not focused day in and day out, and my actions don't back up my commitment.

Our focus determines our action.

In the world of psychology, there is a therapy technique called Cognitive Behavioral Therapy (CBT) which was developed by Dr. Aaron T. Beck. It is used to help people with a variety of mental illnesses by challenging their cognitions (thoughts) which drive their behaviors. If you're saying to yourself, I don't believe all that psychology stuff, then I'll simplify it in a way that we all can agree on. If you tell yourself there is no way you could accomplish _____ (you fill in the blank), (i.e. pass that test, get that job, ask that girl out on a date, make that shot, etc.) you will never accomplish that thing. Your thought about your inability to accomplish that goal will stop you from accomplishing that goal.

The Four Minute Mile

Let's look at an athletic story to drive the point home and talk about the mile run. We all had to do it multiple times in our P.E. classes throughout middle school and high school. The mile was a distance set forth as the measurement we know it today by the Parliament of England in 1593. The measurement is 1760 yards. An article in the Harvard Business Review by Bill Taylor entitled "What Breaking the 4-Minute Mile Taught Us About the Limits of Conventional Thinking" discusses the history of trying to seriously break that barrier began back in 1886. It wasn't done until 1954 when Roger Bannister ran a mile in 3:59.4 seconds. It took 68 years for that feat to be accomplished. British journalist John Bryant had written "For years milers had been striving against the clock, but the elusive four minutes had always beaten them. It had become as much a psychological barrier as a physical one. And like an unconquerable mountain, the closer it was approached, the more daunting it seemed."

The interesting thing is that once the barrier was broken, 46 days later Australian runner John Landy became the second man to run a mile in under four minutes with a time of 3:58 seconds. A year after that three runners did it in the same race. Now more than a 1,000 runners have accomplished what was once thought to be impossible (Taylor, 2018).

It took so long to break that four minute mark, because everyone thought it couldn't be done. However once it was done it began to happen all the time. That is the power of cognition or thought or belief affecting our behavior or actions.

In Mark 9:23 (New King James Version) Jesus makes a statement to a man who was asking if Jesus could do anything to help his son. Jesus said to him "If you can believe, all things are possible to him who believes." Jesus was able, but the key was the man's belief.

Do we limit our lives and what God can do through us due to the lens of what we believe is possible?

One of the definitions of focus is an act of concentrating interest or activity on something. In essence it is giving it our full attention. It is giving of our heart or our will to something. Roger Bannister was able to beat the four minute mile mark because of his focus to accomplish what others believed was impossible. That is the difference in making a commitment and then following up that commitment with your focus, giving it ALL your heart, ALL your soul and ALL your strength (Deuteronomy 6:5).

My Story

Before I go on in this book I would like to tell you my story and where I lost my focus along the way. I grew up in a Christian home. My dad was and still is a pastor. I was the second of four boys. We didn't grow up with a lot of money or things, but I never went without. One of my childhood memories in this regard that I remember was getting my first pair of new pants since all of my clothes were handed down to me from my older brother. I remember asking my mom if it was okay to wear them since they didn't have patches on the knees. She cried when I asked. I wasn't sure why she was crying. I just wanted to make sure I wasn't going to get in trouble for wearing pants without patches. There might not have been a lot of *stuff* in my childhood, but my parents instilled a solid work ethic and respect into their kids for which I am forever grateful.

Another one of my other memories as a young child was trying to keep up with my older brother. This is how the story goes with all second born kids, and especially second born boys with older brothers. The issue with me in this regard is that my older brother is six years older than I am, which I'm sure made me pretty annoying for him. I remember trying to play football with him and his friends in the yard and getting hit and knocked down, but I never wanted to cry. I knew if I cried then they wouldn't let me play with them. I think those years toughened me up a bit. I was a skinny little kid, and I loved to be active. A lot of my punishments given to me by my parents involved me doing exercise (push-ups, jumping jacks, running around the block, etc.). I remember having a conversation with my mom when I was a young boy about heaven. I wanted to know if I had to have a bedtime in heaven or if I could stay up all night playing. I also remember giving up on nap times pretty young as well. I would just stare at the ceiling for an hour or so waiting until I could go outside and play again. When I started going to school I had a difficult time with focusing and getting my assignments done. I remember having to spend the last month of third grade missing every recess, because I hadn't turned in any of my homework since January. My energy level and distractibility made for some challenges in school, but it served me pretty well when my parents allowed me to play organized sports.

I started with soccer and baseball. I loved the feeling of running up and down the soccer field. I'm pretty sure I had no idea what I was doing, but I did love to run. Baseball was fun for a while, but I think I was too hyperactive for the sport. I stopped playing when I was around nine or 10 years old. Somewhere during that time I also started playing basketball, skateboarding and we were constantly playing football in the backyard with other neighborhood kids. It was a fairly normal, or at least what I thought was normal, childhood during that era of time.

I had an opportunity to try out for a club soccer team when I was 10 years old as a goalie, because that's the position they needed not because I had a bunch of experience at it. I was somewhat tall and wasn't afraid to dive and get hit by other players. I played that position for a couple years and did what I could to become the best I could at it. I got some looks from other teams and upper divisions but stuck to my team. I can't say I liked playing goalie all that much, but I knew that was where the team needed me. Eventually as puberty kicked in God blessed me with speed, and the coach felt it was best to move me up to forward. I definitely enjoyed that position much more and threw myself into practicing my dribbling and shooting skills. I would build make shift goals in my backyard and practice and practice and practice. It helped that I grew up in a time before video games and cell phones, because that's all I could really do when I was bored.

Around this time I started to really focus on basketball as well, which I loved. My dad played basketball in college, and he would spend time teaching me how to shoot correctly and do different drills over and over and over. We had a basketball hoop set up in our driveway with a spotlight, and I would practice shooting and dribbling until my parents made me come in and go to bed.

My older brother was a football player, and I was fortunate to grow up in a time where you could try a number of different sports. It seems like nowadays kids have to specialize in one or maybe two sports and that's it. In any case when I got to Middle School I decided to try out for the football team. I told myself I would only play during my Middle School years and then return to soccer when I got to High School. I continued to play on my club soccer team while I played football for my Middle School. I played quarterback and safety. I won the quarterback position through the demanding selection process of the coach having us all line up and see who could throw the ball the furthest. Football was a tougher learning curve for me, and I needed to learn how to get tough and hit other players or I knew I would get hurt and wouldn't last very long. I adapted and really began to enjoy playing that sport as well. I liked the strategy and reading the other teams, and I liked the physicality. I would study my plays and set up objects and tires in my backyard to throw the football at to improve my accuracy. I did pretty well but true to my commitment to myself and after being hazed by my football coaches I returned to soccer when I got into High School.

In 9th grade I played soccer, basketball and track. During that time in our high school league you could only play on the 9th grade team regardless of how good you were. You couldn't play JV or varsity. Our soccer team in 9th grade went undefeated, and the team consisted mostly of the players on my club team. That year in basketball I missed the first two practices of the season due to going hunting. I informed my coach about the hunting trip well in advance, but he seemed upset about it and questioned my level of commitment to the team. For the entire season he never started me in any of the games despite telling me that I was the best shooter he had on the team. I tried to not let it get to me too much, but it did put a bad taste in my mouth for that season and the sport moving forward.

When I got into 10th grade I started playing on the varsity soccer team until I sustained a recurring ankle injury. I never really got back to that starting spot during that season. Two other things occurred during that time in my life. I got a part-time job on the weekends at a restaurant, and I started to pursue girls. I had noticed girls before and did some silly little boyfriend-girlfriend stuff but nothing serious. This was different. I realized now that I could date older girls who were able to drive, and it opened a whole new world to me. This is the point where I started to lose my focus. With the newfound revelation of the female species and my not so fun season with basketball the year before I decided to give up on playing basketball in my 10th grade year, and I never went back. I found out years later that this upset my younger brother who was looking forward to us playing together in high school, and I now do look back with some regret that that never happened.

It probably wasn't the biggest issue that I stopped playing basketball, since I was involved in so many other things and was still a two sport athlete, however the issue is I went too far in my pursuit of girls. It wasn't the first time I struggled sexually. I had been exposed to sexual sin and pornography and had plenty of impure thoughts for some time, but now I was acting on them. I could hear the Holy Spirit speaking to me, coaching me, telling me to stay away. I kept pushing that voice away and temptation turned into sin. I didn't flee (1 Corinthians 6:18) or resist (James 4:7). In fact I learned to ignore the voice. It didn't mean that God didn't stop pursuing me and speaking to me, but I stopped listening.

In James 1:13-15 (New International Version) it says "When tempted, no one should say, 'God is tempting me.' For God cannot be tempted by evil, nor does he tempt anyone; but each person is tempted when they are dragged away by their own evil desire and enticed. Then, after desire has conceived, it gives birth to sin; and sin, when it is full-grown, gives birth to death."

I veered off of God's game plan, lost my focus and got trapped in sin. My whole life was off kilter. I became addicted and began to lose my relationship with God. I felt helpless and unable to stop myself. This pattern went on for a few years and during that time was the first and only time in my life I thought it would be better if I wasn't alive. I allowed myself to be "dragged away" by my own desire. The desire gave birth to sin, and that sin became a pattern that I felt powerless to walk away from. In fact having sex felt like the only thing that took away that pit in my stomach, but it only lasted for a minute and the cycle started over. That is the definition of addiction. God was constantly calling me to repent and walk away, but my thinking was twisted. I couldn't get free. As a therapist I often revisit this time in my life when I listen to others' stories. It helps me to remember that all of us are only one decision away from falling into that trap, and we need to remain humble towards one another.

I was able to stay on track enough with school and work and sports for the most part, but I'm not sure I had the same drive as I did before. I was distracted, which is an understatement. And that is what happens to a lot of us. For me it was sexual sin. It was lust that I allowed to take over and get me off track. For you it might be something else. Pride? Work? Hobbies? Affairs? Emotional affairs? Pornography? Alcohol? Food? Money? Status? Concerns of this world? We have to understand that the devil knows how to trip us up if we let him. He knows how to get us off track just enough, but overtime it leads to our destruction. The devil is an equal opportunity deceiver. He doesn't care where you come from or what you know or who you know or don't know or how much money you have or don't have, and we need to know the enemy we face if we are going to keep our focus.

So not to belabor my story much longer, as I mentioned earlier I was able to graduate high school and secure some partial scholarships to a small college in New York. When I started the preseason training camp for the soccer team I was able to get some distance from things and began to wrestle with the patterns in my life at the time. I was also able to make some friends during that year and chose to be vulnerable about my struggles. I was not able to do this during my battle with lust in the previous years. I was a pastor's kid and lived in fear that if anyone ever found out what I was doing there would be major repercussions for my dad's job, so I kept it a secret. That's another deception of the devil. He wants us to keep our sins hidden and keep us isolated.

James 5:16 (New King James Version) says "Confess your trespasses to one another, and pray for one another, that you may be healed. The effective, fervent prayer of a righteous man avails much." I believe it is noteworthy that in this verse confessing and praying are the two prerequisites or steps to our healing from sin. I confessed my shortcomings to a few close friends who listened and helped me through it and eventually to my parents. I was definitely afraid of talking to my folks, but they loved me and prayed for me. I remember my dad saying to me that the hard part was going to be not returning to my old sin patterns which was definitely true.

So these truths allowed me to let God back in to begin the healing process. It took a couple of years to be honest. The first year was breaking off relationships which weren't good for me, and the second year the Spirit was telling me I needed to take a break from girls for a while to regain my perspective and get back on God's plan. I needed to surrender and spend time listening to God, so He could guide me in this area. So as a sophomore in college I prayed about it, and God spoke to me about not getting physically involved with girls for a year. This was no easy directive for me, but I stayed committed to it in any case. I took the time to work on my own insecurities, and God was true to His word. He gave me a new perspective. I can't say that I automatically started dating the right people, but I was able to tell pretty quickly when a relationship wasn't right for me and had the confidence to walk away.

It wasn't too long after all of this that God brought my wife-to-be Jaime into my life, and I felt His peace over that relationship. I'm not going to lie though. It wasn't easy staying focused on what God wanted for me in that relationship. Old habits die hard. I pushed the boundaries at times but was quick to confess and pray. I didn't allow the sin to grow. The other thing I did during this time in my life was I got baptized. I wanted to make a public declaration in front of God and my church that I was committing myself to refocus on Him and His plan for me.

It has not all been sunshine and roses ever since. I am not going to sit here and tell you that I have never struggled with sexual sin again once I made those decisions. I still struggle with it, however God is faithful and has given me tools for the battle that I'll discuss later in this book. My struggle with the flesh reminds me of when God is talking to Cain after rejecting his sacrifice in Genesis 4: 7 (New International Version) where it says "If you do what is right, will you not be accepted? But if you do not do what is right, sin is crouching at your door; it desires to have you, but you must rule over it." The mental picture of sin crouching at your door like a tiger waiting to pounce on you helps me to focus. I'm not perfect, and I need God's grace every minute of the day to "rule over it."

Here is an illustration of this sin pattern outlined in James 1:14-15, and how God wants us to respond from the verses mentioned earlier:

Temptation (All of us are tempted. Temptation itself is not a sin.)

Desire (We notice we want that sin. It's enticing.) → **Flee** (At this point we need to run.)

Sin (We act upon the desire.) → **Repent** (Confess to God and others and turn back to wisdom.)

Death (A pattern of unrepentant sin) → **Repent** (Turn back to God.)

Losing Our Focus

An issue for me and many of us today in losing our focus is that we live in a day and age of too much information. We can't escape it. Everything we need or want to know about anything is in the palm of our hands or sits on the phone in the pocket of our pants. All of this technology is designed to make our lives easier and more efficient. The commercials tell us that if we use their latest device that we will have more time to spend with our friends and families. It all seems like a great idea. I am just as guilty as the next guy. I have a smart phone in my hand for much of the day checking emails, making phone calls, checking sports scores, social media, etc. I would admit that in some ways it has made my life better, but in many ways it has been very distracting.

We are now connected to our work all the time. Emails and phone calls come in on a constant basis, so at times we feel like we're always at the office. No longer do we come home and leave work at work and spend time with the family. Often we are looking at our phone screens as our wife and children attempt to talk to us. Also the ease of our handheld computers allows us to fall into the devil's trap of extramarital relationships and pornography in a way that is easier than ever before. All of this to say is that there are many more things out in the world today that can distract us (as if we needed any help in that regard).

In athletics, we were extremely focused on the task at hand. We wanted to win the game that week. We wanted to win the championship. We wanted to win, and we worked hard to try and make that happen. We were careful that we ate right, that we got enough sleep and that we kept our grades up so we'd be eligible to play. We were focused on our teammates and how they were doing. We were focused on our coaches and what they were teaching us. We were focused on learning the playbook, so we could execute it on the field. We were singular in our purpose, which made us effective in our mission.

The coach laid out for us what he wanted us to be focused on, so that we would be ready and could perform at our best. If we listened and we worked, we got to play in the game. If we ignored the advice, we ended up on the bench or ineligible to play. It was very clear for us that we needed to remain focused on the game plan. We wouldn't party the night before a game. We made sure to be at practice on time and ready to go. We took care of our responsibilities off the field, so we wouldn't hurt our chances of being able to play. Most of the time it wasn't hard to remain focused, because we didn't want to let our teammates down. We had worked so hard together to get where we were. We put in so many hours in the gym and at practice. We weren't going to throw all of that work away by doing something stupid that would let our teammates down. We held each other accountable to that focus.

So with that in mind we need to ask ourselves, in the game of life which we're playing now, where is my focus?

In Proverbs 4 (New International Version) King Solomon is giving instruction to his sons. He is giving instruction on what should be the focus of their life. He writes:

Listen, my sons, to a father's instruction; pay attention and gain understanding.

I give you sound learning, so do not forsake my teaching.

For I too was a son to my father, still tender, and cherished by my mother.

Then he taught me, and he said to me, "Take hold of my words with all your heart; keep my commandments and you will live. Get wisdom, get understanding; do not forget my words or turn away from them. Do not forsake wisdom, and she will protect you; love her, and she will watch over you. The beginning of wisdom is this: Get wisdom. Though it cost all you have, get understanding. Cherish her, and she will exalt you; embrace her, and she will honor you. She will give you a garland to grace your head and present you with a glorious crown."

Listen, my son, accept what I say, and the years of your life will be many.

I instruct you in the way of wisdom and lead you along straight paths.

When you walk, your steps will not be hampered; when you run, you will not stumble.

Hold on to instruction, do not let it go; guard it well, for it is your life.

Do not set foot on the path of the wicked or walk in the way of evildoers.

Avoid it, do not travel on it; turn from it and go on your way.

For they cannot rest until they do evil; they are robbed of sleep till they make someone stumble.

They eat the bread of wickedness and drink the wine of violence.

The path of the righteous is like the morning sun, shining ever brighter till the full light of day.

But the way of the wicked is like deep darkness; they do not know what makes them stumble.

My son, pay attention to what I say; turn your ear to my words.

Do not let them out of your sight, keep them within your heart; for they are life to those who find them and health to one's whole body.

Above all else, guard your heart, for everything you do flows from it.

Keep your mouth free from perversity; keep corrupt talk far from your lips.

Let your eyes look straight ahead; fix your gaze directly before you.

Give careful thought to the paths for your feet and be steadfast in all your ways.

Do not turn to the right or to the left; keep your foot from evil.

Reading through that chapter it seems pretty clear to me the focus God wants me to have. Look again at some of the verses:

"Hold on to instruction, do not let it go: guard it well, for it is your life." (v. 13)

"My son, pay attention to what I say; turn your ear to my words." (v. 20)

"Let your eyes look straight ahead; fix your gaze directly before you." (v. 25)

"Give careful thought to the paths for your feet and be steadfast in all your ways." (v. 26)

"Do not turn to the right or to the left; keep your foot from evil." (v. 27)

God's word, His instruction, His teaching, and His wisdom are to be our focus. It actually says you are to hold on to it and guard it for it is your life.

Remember our focus determines our action.

God wants us to focus on Him and His plan for our lives every day. In athletics success on the field did not come from a one time commitment to the team, rather from a day in and day out focus and execution of the game plan.

Chapter 3

<u>Where Is Your Game Plan?</u>

"If you aim at nothing you will hit it every time."

-Zig Ziglar

God gave us His playbook on life in the Bible. It is called the word of God, His word to us. The issue is if we only see the Bible as just a collection of historical stories and dos and don'ts that were nice for Sunday school classes but don't have any real application to my life today, then it doesn't do us much good when our marriage is on the edge or we're struggling to get up each day. If I'm able recite John 3:16 and a couple of other verses if someone held a gun to my head, but it doesn't go much further, then what do I do when the game of life gets more difficult? Imagine for a second going into a game scenario and only knowing one play out of the playbook. Could you imagine yourself staring blankly at the coach as he or she is calling out the next play to you and having no idea what the play is? It's unthinkable for you I'm sure. The sad thing is that is the picture of life for a lot of us as Christians. We're lost and staring blankly at God wondering what is going on with our life.

Most of us as Christians believe the Bible to be the word of God, but do we know what it says and how His game plan applies to our lives?

The few years that I played football in middle school was the first time that I understood the importance of a playbook. I was the quarterback for the team but had never played football competitively before. We played our fair share of tackle football in the backyard where you drew the plays up on the palm of your hand, but that was it. As the quarterback of this team it was my job to know all of the plays and positions on the offensive side of the ball. Who was supposed to be where? What hole in the line was the running back going through? Where were the receivers supposed to line up? Was I lined up under center or in a shotgun position? What were the names of all the plays and what did they mean?

It was a lot to take in and learn, and I have to admit that I felt a little overwhelmed at first. The other guys on my team had played for some years before me, and I had some catching up to do. My coach knew I hadn't really played the game before, so he gave me a playbook. He told me to study it and that's what I did. I'm sure it wasn't a very extensive playbook since it was middle school football, but I took it seriously. I realized I needed to know my stuff in order to lead my team on the offensive side of the ball.

What if as Christian men we viewed the Bible and the church the same way we did the practice field and preparing for a game?

As players we went to the practice field daily, if not multiple times a day, worked and pushed ourselves so we could learn and get better at our sport. It was our priority and focus as athletes to be the best we could be for ourselves, our team and our coach. We memorized our playbooks and put in countless hours on the field and in the weight room. Do I view my relationship with God and learning His playbook in the same way? Admittedly I often do not.

In Matthew 6:33 (King James Version) it says "But seek ye first the Kingdom of God, and his righteousness and all these things will be added unto you." It seems pretty clear God wants us to seek Him the same way we prepared ourselves as athletes. He needs me to view that relationship as my top priority. He wants me to put Him first. We can and do gather knowledge about different areas in our life from all kinds of places (TV, internet, friends, family, bosses, school, jobs, etc.), but as the verse says if we want "all these things" to be "added unto" us in our life we need to put Him and His word first.

So what are we giving priority in our life? What are we putting first? What is informing me in my role as a husband, father and employee? What is informing my game plan as a man and a leader?

In our lives God wants our game plan to come from:

1. Prayer- Time spent in relationship and communication with God (The Coach)
2. Bible- Time spent studying and memorizing His word (The Playbook)

So how is the Bible a playbook for the field of life we're in now? And how does prayer provide me with direction for my life?

The word of God gives us instruction on how to live this life, and the house of God trains us in how to apply it. It is the same concept as an athlete. The playbook and communication with the coach gave you the knowledge of what was to be executed on the field, and the practices provided you the opportunity to apply that knowledge in order to be ready for the game.

Understanding the Game

To start off though we need to understand the game we're playing. Just like in athletics you needed to understand what it took to win. What was the objective? What were the rules? The same goes for life now. Honestly it may just be me, but I too often feel like I'm not sure what the rules are and how I play this game. I do however as a Christian have a guide and an example to look to.

In Ephesians 6:10-13 (New King James Version) it sheds some insight into the game we are playing, some of the rules of engagement and how we are to prepare to win. It says "Finally, my brethren, be strong in the Lord and in the power of His might. Put on the whole armor of God, that you may be able to stand against the wiles of the devil. For we do not wrestle against flesh and blood, but against principalities, against powers, against the rulers of the darkness of this age, against spiritual hosts of wickedness in the heavenly places. Therefore take up the whole armor of God, that you may be able to withstand in the evil day, and having done all, to stand."

We are in a battle against the devil and his army. It's hard to know how to win in that game if we don't even realize who we are playing against. We too often end up fighting against our own team, because we don't know who our opponent is. We too often think the enemy is our boss or our spouse or that awful neighbor or my kids who won't listen to me. Jesus provides us with a great example of how to play to win in this game when He is tempted by the devil in the wilderness after fasting for 40 days in preparation for His ministry (Matthew 4:1-11). Yes you read that right. Fasting for 40 days. You see the devil is cunning. He comes after you when you are vulnerable and weak (1 Peter 5:8).

There is a tool that is used in the substance abuse recovery world called the H.A.L.T. (Hungry, Angry, Lonely, Tired) acronym. You *halt* or *stop* and check in with yourself, asking how you're doing with these different feelings. The more of them that you are experiencing the more vulnerable you are to relapsing on drugs or alcohol. I use this tool myself to gauge how I'm doing sometimes and how vulnerable I am to fall into temptation. For me I typically land in the "Lonely and Tired" realms, and the devil comes after me there. However if you ask my wife and kids they'll probably tell you I land in the "Angry" realm too. I imagine Jesus was feeling all four after "Jesus was led by the Spirit to be tempted by the devil" (Matthew 4:1 New King James Version) and went without food for 40 days. It's important to note that the Holy Spirit led Jesus to be tempted by the devil. God the Father was using this experience to prepare His Son for the *game* ahead, similar to an athlete's preseason training.

So how did the devil go after Jesus? How does Jesus respond? What does He do to fight His adversary?

I find it telling in Matthew 4:3 (New King James Version) that when the devil tempts Jesus he makes the statement "If You are the Son of God," as if he didn't know Jesus was the Son of God. Why does he say this? In my opinion the reason he does this sheds insight into how the devil goes after us. He wants us to question who we are. He wants us to question who we are in our relationship with God. The devil wants to plant a seed of doubt. Jesus knows He is the Son of God, but the devil is trying to get Him to question His position. He does the same with us, and we need to remind ourselves daily of whose team we are on and who we are in God. The temptations themselves also shed some light into how the enemy comes after us and how God prepares us for the game. Let's put the three temptations of Jesus into the following categories for further analysis:

1. Flesh
2. Ego
3. Pride

Flesh- "I want what I want"

The devil first tempts Jesus with bread after fasting for 40 days. He says "command that these stones become bread." The devil is appealing to Jesus satisfying his physical flesh, but he is also trying to get Him to doubt that His Father will take care of Him. I almost lose my mind after fasting for a couple of days, so I couldn't imagine 40. In any case I can, as probably all of us can, relate to the desire to satisfy the flesh, be it food or lust or revenge or an addiction of some sort. We all wrestle with it, and we all went through it as athletes as well. During the season and in training we had to deny ourselves all kinds of things we wanted in order to play at our optimal level. So how does Jesus respond to the temptation of His flesh? He responds the same way with each temptation. He quotes from the playbook. He recites scripture. In

Matthew 4:4 (New Living Translation) He says that man lives "by every word that proceeds from the mouth of God." Jesus is quoting from Deuteronomy which mirrors His wilderness experience. The nation of Israel was in the wilderness for 40 years. Jesus was led to the wilderness and fasted for 40 days.

Deuteronomy 8:2-3 (New King James Version)

And you shall remember that the Lord your God led you all the way these forty years in the wilderness, to humble you and test you, to know what was in your heart, whether you would keep His commandments or not. So He humbled you, allowed you to hunger, and fed you with manna which you did not know nor did your fathers know, that He might make you know that man shall not live by bread alone; but man lives by every word that proceeds from the mouth of the Lord.

Jesus quotes the last part of these verses in His response to the devil to deny the temptation of His flesh by recognizing that the Father provides all of His needs. That is the point of why He uses that play from the playbook. He is reminding Himself that God has His back. Jesus is being humbled and tested, but God has Him in His hand. In my own life I try and fulfill fleshly desires often because I don't trust God's plan. I think if I deny myself, then who will take care of me? I want what I want and don't trust God's plan is best, however Jesus trusted God and His word.

Ego- "Look what I can do"

In the second temptation the devil challenges Jesus' position by stating again "If you are the Son of God..." This time he takes Jesus to the top of the temple and challenges Him to jump off saying if you're really God's Son, then the angels will catch you. He is appealing to Jesus' ego. He is taunting Him in a way like a kid at the school yard saying "You think you're so great? Prove it!"

Often times one of the harder things to accomplish as a coach is to be successful when you have a very talented team. How do I get all of these egos to play together? We can all think of some professional athletic teams or teams we played on that seemed stacked with talent but didn't measure up to their potential because all of those egos got in the way.

Jesus responds to the devil in this temptation in Matthew 4:7 (New International Version) by saying "Do not put the Lord your God to the test." He is quoting Deuteronomy 6:16. Jesus understands that His power comes from His relationship with the Father (Matthew 11:27), not from His own greatness. As players we needed to understand that individually we were never better than the team. Jesus refuted the devil by exercising humility and understanding His place and assignment. Jesus does not give Himself credit but gives credit back to the Father. It's not "Look at what I can do," it's giving credit where credit is due (Matthew 5:16).

Pride- "I don't need God"

With the last temptation the devil does *not* start with "If you are the Son of God" this time around. This is significant because the temptation or the challenge no longer works. In James 4:7 (New King James Version) it says "Therefore submit to God. Resist the devil and he will flee from you." Throughout this testing Jesus has not wavered in His position. He has not allowed Himself to doubt that the Father will take care of Him, thus the devil doesn't come after Him in that fashion any longer. The other significant aspect to this is that the devil doesn't give up either. He is looking for a new way to trip Jesus up. It is no different with us.

This time he goes after the thing that is probably the biggest deterrent to God being able to effectively use any of us: pride. In this last temptation the devil offers Jesus all of the kingdoms of the world. All He needed to do was worship him. Some will look at this temptation and label it as materialism, but it goes deeper than that. Inherent in materialism is the sin of pride. It's the thought of look at me and what I'm able to accomplish. Worship me and all the things I've been able to do and get. I don't need God. Pride was the thing that got Satan kicked out of heaven, and pride introduced sin into mankind.

In Psalm 10:4 (New International Version) it states "In his pride the wicked man does not seek him; in all his thoughts there is no room for God." Our pride puts us in a place of focusing on our own self-importance and not focusing on God and others. Pride has ruined many careers, marriages and lives. It sometimes seems like every other week there is a story on the news of celebrities who have killed themselves, and we wonder how they could do that when they have everything this world has to offer. It's kind of interesting that in the last temptation the devil was offering Jesus the same thing, everything the world has to offer. He appealed to Jesus' pride which would have been his eventual undoing if he gave in to it.

32

To combat his opponent this time Jesus uses Deuteronomy 6:13 to repel the devil. He acknowledges that the purpose and focus of His life is to worship and serve God. By doing so He is negating the worship of self and sends the devil packing. Remember that this whole testing of Jesus was initiated by the Holy Spirit (Matthew 4:1). God was preparing His Son for His ministry ahead. God is doing the same with us in addressing these thought processes and heart issues to make sure we are game ready before we step on the field, just like a coach who had to teach us, train us and get us in shape.

Applying the Playbook

So how does God's playbook (the Bible) apply to us in our lives today and the battles we face? If I were to break down the process on the athletic field when it came to how the playbook worked and directed how you as an individual or the team were supposed to operate, I would list it out in the following steps:

1. Study the playbook
2. Memorize the plays
3. Practice the plays
4. Analyze your opponent
5. Call out and execute the play

All of us as athletes can relate to that list. It makes sense in the realm of athletics. So let's take a minute and relate the same steps to God's playbook and the example Jesus set for us in His 40 day testing in the wilderness.

1. **Study the playbook**

As athletes when we were preparing for the season our coach would give us a playbook for us to learn, so that we were speaking the same language on the field. We would have a mutual understanding of what the plays meant and what the coach wanted us to do. God gave us the same thing with the Bible. He wants us to study, so that we know what He expects and what we need to do out on the *field* of life we play on today. In Joshua 1:8 (New Living Translation) it says "Study this Book of Instruction continually. Meditate on it day and night so you will be sure to obey everything written in it. Only then will you prosper and succeed in all you do." As players we studied the playbook because we believed it would give us an advantage in the game. We need to see and study God's playbook in the same way.

2. **Memorize the plays**

It was one thing to study the playbook, but in reality we needed to memorize the plays in that book in order to effectively execute them in the game. On the football or soccer field or the basketball court when the coach called out the play he or she wanted the team to do at that particular moment, we needed to know the plays. We couldn't run to the sideline and grab our playbook and look it up. It's the same with God's word and the necessity of knowing it when we need it. In Deuteronomy 11:18 (Contemporary English Version) it says "Memorize these laws and think about them. Write down copies and tie them to your wrists and your foreheads to help you obey them." If we don't know the plays when it counts it doesn't do us much good. When Jesus was being tempted by the devil in the wilderness He had His *plays* memorized.

3. **Practice the plays**

With anything in life or with people it's not what you say that counts, it's what you do. Actions speak louder than words, as the saying goes. We can know the playbook. We can memorize verses, but it doesn't make any difference for ourselves or for others if we aren't practicing (doing) what it says. Same thing goes on the field as athletes which is why we put in so much time at practice, so that we could execute the plays when it counted. We might not have liked practice at times, but we never thought it would be a good idea to just study the playbook and then jump straight into a game. It would never work.

This concept is illustrated in James 1:22-25 (New King James Version) where it says "But be doers of the word, and not hearers only, deceiving yourselves. For if anyone is a hearer of the word and not a doer, he is like a man observing his natural face in a mirror; for he observes himself, goes away, and immediately forgets what kind of man he was. But he who looks into the perfect law of liberty and continues in it, and is not a forgetful hearer but a doer of the work, this one will be blessed in what he does."

Verse 25 captures the essence of this truth by stating that we need to "continue in it." We need to practice it over and over. Also do not be "a forgetful hearer but a doer of the work." Put in the work. Put in the practice and then "he will be blessed in what he does."

4. Analyze your opponent

In preparation for game day a coach and the players will analyze their upcoming opponent. They'll watch game film and discuss strategies to best match up and beat the other team. They will practice and prepare the week before in specific formations and plays that they feel will best match up against the team they're going to play. This is a common and wise thing to do in order to be game ready. In the wilderness Jesus knew His adversary and knew the plays he would need to run in order to win. In 2 Corinthians 2:11 (New International Version) it says "in order that Satan might not outwit us. For we are not unaware of his schemes."

We need to be aware of "his schemes." How does he get us off track? How does he frustrate us? How does he get in your head and get you off your game? We need to remember how he attacked Jesus as He was preparing for His time of ministry when He was in the wilderness. The devil went after his flesh, ego and pride.

5. Call out and execute the play

With this last step it is now game time, and you're on the field. The coach sees how the other team is lined up and calls out the play he or she wants the team to run. The captain or quarterback or point guard then echoes the coach's command, so that the team knows which play to run. Also sometimes the players in charge will analyze what is happening in the flow of a game and call an audible, meaning they will change the play at the line of scrimmage or on the court where they see a match up discrepancy that is advantageous for the team. These players are so in tune with the coach, the system and the playbook that they begin to think and act like the coach.

The issue here is that if the captain never calls out the play, then the team doesn't know what to do. These players have to say it out loud, not just think it in their head. When Jesus was tempted in the wilderness He called out the play from scripture in order to resist the devil. We can go through all of the steps of studying, memorizing, practicing, and analyzing, but if we never call out the play and execute it, it doesn't matter.

Proverbs 18:21a (English Standard Version) states that "Death and life are in the power of the tongue." We speak over our future. Too often I am speaking the wrong things about myself and those around me. I need to know what God says about the different areas of my life and then speak those things when the enemy comes to steal my focus.

Examples from the Playbook

Let's take a quick look at a few examples of how this works. How does God's game plan operate to fight against our adversary? You identify the attack, speak the play from the playbook against it and then walk it out. The list below is not exhaustive by any means but is a snapshot of God's playbook in regards to some specific areas of our lives.

Feeling hopeless?

"For I know the plans I have for you," declares the Lord, "plans to prosper you and not to harm you, plans to give you hope and a future (Jeremiah 29:11 New International Version)."

"May the God of hope fill you with all joy and peace as you trust in him, so that you may overflow with hope by the power of the Holy Spirit (Romans 15:13 New International Version)."

Feeling anxious?

"Do not be anxious about anything, but in every situation, by prayer and petition, with thanksgiving present your requests to God. And the peace of God, which transcends all understanding, will guard your hearts and minds in Christ Jesus (Philippians 4:6-7 New International Version)."

"Cast all your anxiety on Him because he cares for you (1 Peter 5:7 New International Version)."

"And my God shall supply all your need according to His riches in glory by Christ Jesus (Philippians 4:19 New King James Version)."

Feeling lonely or afraid?

"Be strong and courageous. Do not be afraid or terrified because of them, for the Lord your God goes with you; he will never leave you nor forsake you (Deuteronomy 31:6 New International Version)."

"For God has not given us a spirit of fear; but of power and of love and of a sound mind (2 Timothy 1:7 New King James Version)."

Feeling lost or confused?

"The steps of a good man are ordered by the Lord: and he delighteth in his way. Though he fall, he shall not be utterly cast down: for the Lord upholdeth him with his hand (Psalm 37:23-24 King James Version)."

"Thy word is a lamp unto my feet, and a light unto my path (Psalm 119:105 King James Version)."

"Trust in the Lord with all your heart, And lean not on your own understanding; In all your ways acknowledge Him, And He shall direct your paths (Proverbs 3:5-6 New King James Version).

Feeling persecuted or being treated unfairly?

Bless those who persecute you (Romans 12:9-21).

This one can be especially hard for me when I've been wronged or hurt or am suffering for doing what is right. Sometimes all I can do is to ask for God's help with forgiveness and to simply name the person and ask God to bless them. There has been heartache for sure at times, but I have also seen some amazing things happen that I can only attribute to His working when I obey God in this.

Feeling exhausted?

Don't forget to take a break. As athletes our bodies needed a day off to rest and recover. We need the same in our lives today. God calls it a Sabbath (Exodus 20:8-10).

Are your kids going astray?

"Train up a child in the way he should go, and when he is old he will not depart from it (Proverbs 22:6 New King James Version)."

"There is hope in your future, says the Lord, That your children shall come back to their own border (Jeremiah 31:17 New King James Version)."

What about finances?

If you are able to work, then you need to work (1 Timothy 5:8, 2 Thessalonians 3:10).

Tithe. Give the first ten percent of your earnings to God. Recognize where your job, your ability to work and your provision comes from in order that He will bless the other ninety percent. Be generous and happy to give (Proverbs 3:9-10, Malachi 3:10, 2 Corinthians 9:7, 1 Timothy 6:17-19).

You can't serve both God and money (Matthew 6:24).

Have a financial plan (Luke 14:28-30).

How about my marriage?

Ephesians 5:21-33

How should I treat others?

"Do not judge others, and you will not be judged (Matthew 7:1 New Living Translation)." God alone is the judge (James 4:12), however we are to live with sound judgment (Proverbs 5:14) and discernment (Hebrews 5:14).

"Do nothing out of selfish ambition or vain conceit. Rather, in humility value others above yourselves. (Philippians 2:3 New International Version)"

You have heard that it was said, "You shall love your neighbor and hate your enemy." But I say to you, love your enemies, bless those who curse you, do good to those who hate you, and pray for those who spitefully use you and persecute you, (Matthew 5:43-44 New King James Version)

"So whatever you wish that others would do to you, do also to them, for this is the Law and the Prophets. (Matthew 7:12 English Standard Version)"

"If someone has enough money to live well and sees a brother or sister in need but shows no compassion- how can God's love be in that person? (1 John 3:17 New Living Translation)"

"Each one of you should use whatever gift you have received to serve others, as faithful stewards of God's grace in its various forms (1 Peter 4:10 New International Version)."

God's plan is there for us, but it is up to us to study and learn it each day. In Luke 6:45 (English Standard Version) it says "for out of the abundance of the heart his mouth speaks." Our hearts and minds need to be filled with God's plan, so that we can speak it and use it each day. The plan that we study and put into place in our lives affects how we live out our life. If our plan is to follow the news or the politicians or our bank accounts or our stock portfolios or our favorite sports team or Hollywood or what our neighbors think or the latest thing on social media, then when the trials and tribulations of life come (and they will come as they always do) that is what we will use to combat and get through those difficult times. The problem with the plans of the world is that they often contradict God's plans. In 1 John 2:16 (New Living Translation) it says "For the world offers only a craving for physical pleasure, a craving for everything we see, and pride in our achievements and possessions. These are not from the Father, but are from this world." The world's messages and values encourage us to feed our flesh, ego and pride:

"I want what I want (and it'll also tell you that you deserve it even when it is destructive to you)."

"Look at what I can do (my worth and value is based upon my accomplishments and image, not upon humility and service to others)."

"I don't need God (in fact the world will tell you the things of God are actually holding you back)."

Most of us have heard the statement "The heart wants what it wants" or "Just follow your heart," and this has become a rationale for our decision making and planning in life. People will ask you "What is your heart telling you to do?" when you are facing a decision in life. This rationale however has caused many to stumble and make some foolish decisions in their life. The scriptures warn us in Jeremiah 17:9-10 (English Standard Version) that "The heart is deceitful above all things and desperately sick; who can understand it? I the Lord search the heart and test the mind, to give every man according to his ways, according to the fruit of his deeds." Even in the world of psychology in what is known as Dialectical Behavior Therapy (DBT) patients are encouraged to use their Wise Mind, which is the integration of their Emotional Mind and their Logical Mind, when facing difficulties.

But this still begs the question as to where their source of wisdom is coming from. Is it just the sum of my experiences and knowledge or is it something higher than that?

Karl Marx is famously quoted as calling religion "the opium of the people." I don't know about you, but the longer I'm on this planet I am seeing that our phones and devices and the constant stream of information and media has truly become our opiate. Just take a look around you at any airport or restaurant or even family dinner table, and you will notice almost everyone is looking at their phone. We have access to unlimited knowledge but are we any wiser? We are supposedly more enlightened, but it feels like the world is becoming a darker place. We need to understand that what we fill our time with is what fills our hearts, and the adversary knows this truth as well. I'm not insinuating that we shouldn't be responsible with our finances or live under a rock and not know what is going on in the world, quite the contrary. What I am saying is that we need to be careful and put God's word and His plans as the first priority in our life (Matthew 6:33).

God gave us His word, His manual for life, His playbook, so that we would be successful and blessed while we are living on this planet. Our spiritual maturity in life is based upon our ability to use His word to address the challenges we face, just as our success on the field came from honing our skill and being able to execute the plan our coaches gave us. We had a playbook to study, memorize, practice and apply so that we would be game ready, and God wants the same for us when we step on the field every day of our lives.

A final thought to consider in this regard is that none of us as parents would tell our kids to *not* study for a test they had in school. We would tell them they had to study, get prepared and apply what they learned in order to be successful. God is trying to tell us the same thing.

PART 2
(WHAT)

Chapter 4

<u>What Is a Good Coach?</u>

"A coach is someone who can give correction without causing resentment."

-John Wooden

For this next part of the book I want to take a look at the qualities of a good coach and in the subsequent chapter those of a good player. By investigating these qualities it will help us better understand how God wants to help us and guide us in our journey through life, and the character He is trying to develop in us. I had a conversation with my dad once talking about how some people do really well with a coach but seem to struggle with a boss. I have been a manager and supervisor at different jobs in my life and have also coached for many years. Both a boss and a coach want something. They both want people to be productive and perform at their best. The difference I see is that a boss wants something *from* you for the benefit of the company, whereas a coach wants something *for* you for the benefit of the team. God is like a coach in that way, however I feel like a lot of Christians and non-Christians get that twisted. They see God as a boss to whom they can never measure up, who always wants something more. That is not God. God gave everything *for* us and wants to walk alongside us through life to help us. He wants us to grow and improve as His *players* in order to influence and benefit the world around us. Jesus also sets this standard for his team of disciples when he addresses them in John 13:35 (New King James Version) saying "By this all will know that you are My disciples, if you have love for one another."

So let's look at some aspects of a good coach and see how they connect to the character of God:

<u>Pushes You to Reach Your Potential</u>

"Leave me alone coach," said one of my players as the team was running sprints at the end of practice, and he was refusing to run anymore. My response was "Sometimes I wish I could, but I can't because you're on my team. It's my job to push you." If we're honest, most of us are pretty lazy by nature. Would we go to work if we didn't need the money? Probably not. A lot of us know we need to exercise and eat right, but we don't do it, which is why we have a multi-billion dollar diet and exercise industry. There aren't that many self-motivated people and players out there, and even those that are probably didn't start that way. Someone invested in them and ingrained that value into their being. They had someone in their life that didn't let them get away with mediocrity or complacency. They pushed them beyond what they thought they could do.

I have a photocopy of a devotional from the book *Morning Rounds*, which is a compilation of daily devotionals written by students, faculty, friends and alumni of Loma Linda University School of Medicine that hangs on the wall in my office at work. The devotional was written by Samuel McCash, M.D., and it was about the one day during his residency where he worked in the HIV clinic in San Bernardino, CA where I have been working for the past 13 years. The devotional was about one of my coworkers who I had the pleasure to work beside for the first few years of my employment there and who made a profound impact in my career to this day, Harvey Elder, M.D. The following is an excerpt from that devotional:

I was afraid to say anything- afraid of uttering something wrong and asking questions that might me look as ignorant as I probably was. His face was stern like the pastor of a church. I felt that, sometime during the day, he was going to sit me down and start preaching to me about the righteous and unrighteous acts of life.

All of that changed, however, throughout the day when I saw him with his patients. There was the heroin addict, who had contracted HIV from sharing needles. There was the homosexual man, who needed his medications adjusted and some anal warts removed. There was also the noncompliant patient, who had been in and out of prison, whose only excuse was that she kept forgetting. It was remarkable to see the demeanor of this stern-appearing doctor melt into compassion and care as he dealt with these patients, with these "people."

He never condemned them for their practices, never looked down on them. He was only stern about what the patients had to do for their well-being. His one goal was simple- to get these souls to their next birthday. His arsenal was also very simple: anti-HIV drugs, education, and prayer. The prayer was the most profound to me.

For the first time in medical school, I felt that I was seeing the true love of God. He did not judge them. He did not even speak of the practices that brought them into this place. He met them where they were, trying to give them a second chance at life. That day I saw Jesus, and the place where all of us Christians should be (McCash, 2008, p. 309).

Due to staff contract restructuring Dr. Elder was unable to continue working for the San Bernardino County Public Health Department and transferred to another clinic. I remember listening to him talk about his time working at Public Health at a lunch we had to honor him and say our good-byes, and I can remember it like it was yesterday God asking me, "Who is going to pray for my people now?" The Coach was asking me to step up to the plate. I remember driving home that day and arguing with Him about how I worked at a government facility in California and could possibly lose my job for doing that. I stated my case that Dr. Elder could get away with praying for patients, since his children were grown, and he was basically retired. He only needed to work part-time or was just doing it to give himself something to do. This was my full-time job. I needed this job to feed my family. I also remember God's rebuttal back to me when He asked "What's more important to you, Me or that job? Who do you think got you that job?"

I sat on it for a while but knew God was wanting me to step out in faith. He needed me to take the baton and run my leg of the race. I committed to getting to it and began to ask patients if I could pray for them after I was done meeting with them. I reasoned if there were going to be patient complaints about me doing that and I lost my job, then God would open another door for me. Honestly I was quite nervous and felt really awkward for quite some time. The devil tried to talk me out of it every time I went into an exam room. I needed to push through that with God's help. I likened that time in my career to a coach pushing you to reach your potential. You start off pretty slow and weak, but after putting in the work with the coach's guidance and plan, you get better and stronger. A decade later I am still praying for patients. There are some that refuse the prayer, but easily the majority of my patients accept it and many remind me to do it before I leave the exam room.

I pray for their specific concerns, physically, mentally or relationally, and I ask Him to bless them and their families. I have seen firsthand the power and healing of those prayers. Many patients have talked to me about how those prayers have profoundly helped them. God has given me a line over the years that I close my prayer with and I also pray it over myself and my family each day. "And may His grace, peace, love, strength and encouragement go with you today." This was an area of my faith walk that I needed to develop, and God needed me to step up and continue Dr. Elder's work and legacy with these patients. Those prayers have been an amazing blessing to so many hurting and marginalized people over the years, and they never would have happened if God didn't push me to reach my potential in that area. That is what a good coach did for us on the athletic field, and that is what God wants to do for us if we allow Him to and obey Him in the process.

The issue for a lot of us, myself included, and the player on my team that I mentioned earlier is that it takes pain and suffering in order to grow and get better. None of us like pain and suffering, and we need a coach to push us through that in order for us to reap the reward on the other side. In Romans 5:3-4 (New International Version) it says "Not only so, but we also glory in our sufferings, because we know that suffering produces perseverance; perseverance, character; and character, hope." As people we want to have more character and hope in our lives, but we need to understand that those things come from suffering and perseverance. A good coach walks alongside us, pushes us and encourages us to reach our potential through suffering and perseverance that we wouldn't have gotten to on our own.

Provides Vision

Back when I played college soccer, we had a coach in my freshman year that met with the team at the beginning of the season and asked what our goals were as a team. This coach had a proven track record, having won a number of national championships with another college he coached previously. He had also won a national championship as a player and played professionally in the past. We discussed as a team and came up with various goals including winning multiple national championships and producing players each year that would go on to play at the professional level. That year we only lost once during the regular season against the team that eventually won the national title, and we finished fifth in the nation as I had mentioned earlier in the book. We had a few members of that graduating class go on to play at the professional level. We were beginning to fulfill some our goals and beginning to develop a vision for our team and program. Unfortunately that coach was only with us for one season and accepted another position elsewhere, but that meeting at the beginning of that season has always stuck with me. That coach provided a vision for that team and got us as players to start thinking bigger.

In Proverbs 29:18a (King James Version) it says, "Where there is no vision, the people perish." Having a vision in life is extremely important. When I meet with my patients we often discuss short-term and long-term goals. I have them write out their goals in the following increments: one week, one month, three months, six months, one year, two years, and five years. I encourage them to post that paper somewhere they can see it as a reminder to them on a daily basis where they want to be headed in their life. In Habukkuk 2:2 (English Standard Version) it says "Write the vision; make it plain on tablets, so he may run who reads it."

Having a vision and goals gives us a path to run. A good coach does that for his team. He will provide that for his team and for each individual player. The team will know what the goals are for the season ahead and the bigger picture of why they are pushing so hard each day at practice. A good coach will also meet with each of his players individually and discuss a vision and plan to help that player improve in their athletic career.

There is a story in the Bible in 2 Chronicles 24 that illustrates this pretty well. The story is about Joash, who was the king of Judah at the time, and the priest Jehoiada. Now Joash was only seven years old when he became king, and if I can think back to when any of my children were seven years old I definitely wouldn't have wanted them to be ruling a kingdom of any kind. Some of them could barely tie their shoes. So obviously Joash needed some help. He needed some coaching. He needed vision. He received that from his relationship with Jehoiada. In verse 2 (New International Version) it says "Joash did what was right in the sight of the Lord all the days of Jehoiada the priest." There is something very telling in that verse that you might have missed. Joash did what was right *all the days of Jehoiada the priest*. As long as Joash was getting the vision from his *coach*, he was doing good things and going somewhere.

The chapter goes on to tell about how Joash had a vision to repair the house of the Lord. He set out goals to gather the money necessary to complete the job. He meets with Jehoiada to discuss how progress towards the goal was going and to come up with alternative measures to reach the goal when things aren't progressing as planned. Eventually they fund and accomplish the task.

Now here comes the rub in the story. At 130 years old Jehoiada dies and without his guidance Joash abandons the things of God. Various prophets come to try and talk some sense into the king and even Jehoiada's son Zechariah comes to meet with the leaders of Judah. Zechariah's counsel is not heeded, and upon the command of king Joash, he is stoned to death.

Joash did not finish well. He abandoned the vision that was laid out for him and his team (the kingdom of Judah). Soon after the death of Zechariah, the Syrian army defeated Judah, and Joash was injured in battle. Then his *teammates* turned on him. In verse 25 (New King James Version) it says "his own servants conspired against him because of the blood of the sons of Jehoiada the priest, and killed him on his bed."

Jehoiada provided vision and coaching for Joash. He provided him with a goal, a mission and met with him to discuss how he was progressing towards meeting that goal. Jehoiada was the chief priest. He was God's representative to the people. God has a vision for our lives today. He has a specific mission and objective for your life and for mine. We need to stay close to the Coach to better understand that plan and walk it out.

In I John 2:3-6 (New King James Version) it says "Now by this we know that we know Him (know the Coach and His vision), if we keep His commandments (execute the game plan). He who says, 'I know Him,' and does not keep His commandments, is a liar, and the truth is not in him. But whoever keeps His word, truly the love of God is perfected in him. By this we know that we are in Him. He who says he abides in Him ought himself also to walk just as He walked."

Cares for and Encourages His Players

I maybe should have discussed this trait first, but in order for a player to fully respond to a coach's training or to get on board with his or her vision that player needs to know that the coach cares. Does that coach want the best for me? Does that coach check in with me? Does that coach notice the areas I am doing well in and talk to me about the areas I need to improve? Does that coach know anything about me more than just what I do on the field each day?

There are many different coaching styles. Some are loud and in your face. Some are more subdued and calm. Each has their advantages and disadvantages, but in order for players to truly respond and give their all they need to know that the person with the whistle or yelling from the sideline wants the best for them. I believe coaches have a unique opportunity to speak into players' lives and have a profound ministry impact that I will talk more about in Chapter 11.

That care and encouragement goes beyond the practices and the games. A good coach has the ability to speak life into their players. They can see their potential and get their players to as well. They have relationships with their players. They know how things are going at home or at school or in their friendships. All of this provides a framework of trust and respect.

Jurgen Klopp is the current manager (coach) for the Liverpool Football Club (soccer for us Americans). He has been in this position since 2015. Since taking over he has taken his team to the UEFA Champions League finals in 2018 and 2019, winning it in 2019. He also won the English Premier League title in 2020 and finished second in 2019, as well as being named the FIFA Coach of the Year in 2019 and 2020. Needless to say he is a pretty good coach. The following is an excerpt from an interview with him:

> "Apart from sleeping, I think the whole day- in fact probably when I am sleeping- about those boys (his players). I don't want to, it just happens because there is so much information you have.
>
> For me the most important thing is for the player to be in his best shape in the moment when it counts and we try to do that with nutrition, training and tactics.
>
> But there is a time when they go home and there is still a situation. That is normal life but it all influences performance.
>
> I don't pretend I'm interested. I am interested. It's important to know who you are working with and it's important to know why somebody is determined and motivated.
>
> I think I need to know them. That's what creates a relationship. They can talk to me and it's always important (Jurgen Klopp explains how he cultivates his incredible relationship with players, 2020)."

When you look at the words behind what Coach Klopp is saying, that reflects the heart of God towards us:

1. Klopp says he thinks about his players all the time. In Psalm 137:17-18 (New Living Translation) it says "How precious are your thoughts about me, O God. They cannot be numbered! I can't even count them; they outnumber the grains of sand! And when I wake up, you are still with me!" God is always thinking about us as well, and His thoughts towards us are higher than our thoughts (Isaiah 55:9).
2. Coach Klopp trains his players to be ready for when it counts in the game. In Psalm 144:1 (English Standard Version) it says "Blessed be the Lord, my rock, who trains my hands for war, and my fingers for battle;" God also wants us to be ready for when it counts in life. He does this through His word by teaching, rebuking, correcting and training, so that we are thoroughly equipped (2 Timothy 3:16-17).
3. As problems come up in the lives of his players, Coach Klopp is interested and listens. He has a relationship with his players, and whatever concerns them is very important to him. In Psalm 18:6 (English Standard Version) it says "In my distress I called upon the Lord; to my God I cried for help. From his temple he heard my voice, and my cry to him reached his ears."

For a long time in my life I didn't think of God as caring or encouraging. I saw Him and our relationship as one where if I followed the rules, then He would leave me alone. It set up for me a pretty legalistic view of my faith and the somewhat pervasive thought process out there that Christianity is just a bunch of *dos and don'ts*. Also as I went further into my addictive sin pattern I felt like God was always mad at me. I could never measure up, and all I did was let Him down. When I eventually understood that He loved me and just wanted what was best for me it changed our whole relationship. I didn't get better overnight, but I became more open about my shortcomings and seeking Him for help. I became more open to His coaching (teaching, rebuking, correcting and training) and obeying what He was wanting me to do in order to be in the "best shape in the moment when it counts."

Gives Clear Direction

When it comes to the concept of God *coaching* us, He is giving us clear direction on how we are to live our lives. We then choose if we listen to and follow that direction. If we think about it from the world of athletics, we would not consider a coach who didn't provide his or her players with direction to be a very good coach. Just imagine showing up to practice and your coach throws some balls out on the field or the court and says "Grab a ball and get better at the game!" You could practice some techniques you've learned or watched before, but that hands-off approach isn't going to take you very far. Players sign scholarship agreements with elite collegiate programs or compete to join certain athletic programs as a youth or as a professional, because the coaching staff can provide them with the instruction and training to become the best players they can be.

The same is true for God and the direction He wants to provide for our lives. God's playbook is very specific, and so are His plan and purpose for your life. In 1 Corinthians 14:33 (New King James Version) it says "For God is not the author of confusion, but of peace, as in all the churches of the saints." Furthermore it says in Philippians 2:13 (New International Version) "for it is God who works in you to will and to act to fulfill his good purpose." His plan for us is to bring His goodness to the world, "to fulfill his good purpose." A coach who just tosses a bunch of balls out on to a field and tells his team to figure it out causes *confusion*. A coach who has a specific plan for the team and works with them to play it out brings *peace*. The coach's direction and plan allows the players "to will and to act to fulfill" the "good purpose" of that team.

Let's take a little deeper look into the areas God directs us through His playbook in order to get us ready as His players as laid out in 2 Timothy 3:16-17 (New International Version) where it says:

All Scripture is God-breathed and is useful for *teaching, rebuking, correcting and training* in righteousness, so that the servant of God may be thoroughly equipped for every good work.

Teaching:

In order to get better at anything in sports and anything in life for that matter we needed someone to teach us. We needed someone at home, at school, on the job, etc. We needed someone to walk us through what we needed to do. We needed to watch someone walk it out or model it to us. For us as Christians this is why the life and teachings of Jesus is so important, because we have an example of how we are to live out our faith. In the athletic world a good coach will show his players how to play and perform on the field as well. He or she will discuss and demonstrate the proper mechanics of a certain skill or play, however before any of that can be done a coach needs to teach his team what the rules and expectations are for the game and for the team. The process is no different when you start a new job. You have to learn the policies and procedures and culture of the place first before you jump into your assigned position. You might have a new employee orientation or class of some sort which lays that all out for you.

God desires to do the same for us in every area of our lives (relationships, health, marriage, children, finances, business, etc.). In Psalm 32:8 (English Standard Version) it says "I will instruct you and teach you in the way you should go; I will counsel you with my eye upon you." God wants to teach us the way we should go. He wants to lay out His expectations for us and give us a path to success. His eye is also upon us in this process. God is not disinterested and apathetic towards us. He is watching our lives just like a coach watches his or her players.

Rebuking:

So what happens when a player doesn't listen to or follow the rules of the team? Or a team isn't giving the effort they need to in practice or in the game? Or the team doesn't listen to or ignores what the coach is saying? Or the team starts to argue and fight amongst itself? Does a good coach let it slide or let it go? Of course not. A good coach steps in, intervenes and holds his players accountable to the team standard. The team standard is the same set of rules and expectations which apply to every player.

The word rebuke is not something we use a lot in our everyday conversations these days but in terms of language we do use it can be defined as taking someone to task or an expression of disapproval. As a coach I tend to come on strong in the beginning. I let my players know up front in the first practice what my expectations are and what will happen if they don't listen. I come from the thought process that it is harder to be lenient in the beginning and then try to rein things in later on, especially with coaching children and adolescents.

Some of the rules I lay out from day one is that when I call for the team to circle up and listen, then I expect that is done right away. I expect that when I am talking that they are not talking. I tell them that I will not tolerate trash talk, disrespect and cursing on my team. There are reasons for these rules. I can't teach if I have to compete with everyone else's voices. Practices are only so long, so I have limited time to accomplish what I need to do with them. Also a house divided against itself cannot stand (Mark 3:25), so if my players start trash talking each other it is very hard for them to unify as a team. My consequences are quick and immediate typically in the form of push-ups or running laps. Sometimes those consequences are individually doled out and sometimes the whole team does them. My goal is to instill team discipline and respect. This may sound harsh to some of you who are reading this, but these rebukes come from a place of love and care that I have for my players. I am not demeaning or disrespectful to them. I have a standard for their behavior, attitude and interactions that I expect from them. On the flip side I have seen teams with a ton of talent that couldn't come together or win, because their coach was too interested in being their friend as opposed to holding his players accountable, which created a chaotic team culture.

In Proverbs 13:1 (New International Version) it says "A wise son heeds his father's instruction, but a mocker does not respond to rebukes." As coaches we have all had that player who is a "mocker" on our team. It throws everything off and can be very difficult to maintain your team identity and culture. Sometimes we are that "mocker," and God rebukes us as well to get us back in line with His team standard. I have definitely been that player on God's team at times, and He has needed to rebuke me pretty sternly. He does this for our sake and for the sake of His team. Teams run into trouble when players go rogue, stop listening to the coach and start doing things their own way.

Correcting:

There is a difference between rebuke and correction. Rebuking from a coaching standpoint addresses the bigger issues that evolve when an individual player or team as a whole knowingly violate the rules or expectations of that team. That individual or individuals need to be taken to task in order for the team culture or that player to remain healthy and productive. This would also be the case in a family or in a business as a manager with employees who are disrupting those systems. Correction can be seen as fine tuning. The team is now on board with the standard and rules of the coach. Some rebukes are still necessary from time to time, but it is definitely less frequent. It is at this time when a coach can begin to truly prepare his team for the game.

When I begin a season of coaching I work on the team's fitness, but I also run them through a series of drills in order to see their level of skill and ability at the different techniques and mechanics necessary for the game and their position on the team. I often have to address technique and form issues and work on my players unlearning improper or poor habits they have picked up over the years. This is where correction begins. My players are already on board with the team standard. I am not fighting them to line up or to listen or to stop talking or to stop arguing with each other. At this point as a coach I can begin to truly instruct my players. It is the same for God with us. We can begin to be improved and equipped by God for our role on His team only after we get on board with His standard. We have to choose to do God's will God's way, not our way. Too often in my own life and in the stories I listen to I hear Christians who want to do life their own way, instead of God's plan and still expect Him to get behind it and bless them. We all know a good coach wouldn't allow that from one of his players and would expect his or her team to practice and play the strategy and tactics the coach sets forth for the team.

In this time of correction I inevitably have players who fight against me and my fine tuning saying something like "But coach this is how I've always done it, and it's worked pretty good so far." I try to explain that those improper techniques might work for now, but when the competition gets tougher and the game gets faster you won't be able to keep up. This is where you begin to notice the different levels of how coachable a particular player is. Does that player trust the coach, listen and change or does that player continue to do what he or she has always done?

In Proverbs 15:32 (New International Version) it says "Those who disregard discipline despise themselves, but the one who heeds correction gains understanding." God is doing the same thing when it comes to coaching you and me. He sees the areas of our lives that need to be unlearned or improved. He sees the bad habits or improper thought processes and blows the whistle for us to stop, so He can instruct us. God then begins to tell us to do this or that or don't do this or that or approach this in a different way. How coachable am I in those moments? Do I tell God that "this is how I've always done it, and it's worked pretty good so far?" Or do I heed correction to gain understanding? God, just like our coaches, sees the competition ahead and is trying to prepare us for it. The way I did things before won't work when the game of life gets harder. I need to change and begin to practice what He is telling me to do.

Training:

It is only after I have an understanding of the teaching, have responded to the rebukes and have heeded correction that I can begin to train. I am now on board with the rules and expectations. I am willing to unlearn improper techniques. And lastly I am beginning to perform and execute those skills in the way they are supposed to be done. It is at this point that a coach can really train his or her team. It is now when all of the workout regimens, nutrition plans and drills begin to work and take shape in each individual player and the team as a whole. Individualized training plans are tailored to each player's needs, and the team begins to connect the plays and strategies and correctly execute them. The players and the team begin to think and act like the coach and his or her game plan.

It is similar to our spiritual walk and God's coaching of us. We gain a knowledge of His teaching through His word. We listen to His rebukes and corrections and repent of the ways we have been doing things. He helps us to unlearn our sin patterns and shows us a better way to do life. From that point we can start to live out life God's way, training ourselves to think and act like Him. This last point is illustrated in Luke 6:40 (New International Version) where it says "The student is not above the teacher, but everyone who is fully trained will be like their teacher."

Puts the Right Players Around You

Michael Jordan is considered by many, if not most, people to be the best basketball player of all time. His Chicago Bulls team dominated the NBA in the 1990s, winning three consecutive championships twice in that decade. Jordan was drafted with the third overall pick by the Bulls in 1984. Jordan was able to lead the team back to the playoffs in his rookie year, losing to the Milwaukee Bucks in four games. In his second year the Bulls made the playoffs again, this time they were swept by the Boston Celtics. In his third year in the league the team was swept again in the first round of the playoffs by the Celtics despite Jordan scoring 3,041 points that year, which was the highest amount in his career. That point total also made him only the second player in NBA history besides Wilt Chamberlain to score over 3,000 points in a season. Needless to say Jordan was playing quite well in his first three years in the NBA but never made it out of the first round of the playoffs.

It wasn't until the 1987-1988 season when the Bulls drafted Scottie Pippen and Horace Grant that they began to have playoff success. The championships didn't come right away. They would lose to the Detroit Pistons in the playoffs in the next three seasons, but they were able to get out of the first round and then made the Eastern Conference Finals in 1989 and 1990. It was from there that the Bulls would go on to dominate the league until 1998. It was obvious from Jordan's rookie year that he was a special player. His talent and drive were incredible, however he didn't have real success until the right players were put around him. In fact Scottie Pippen was his teammate for all six of those championships.

A good coach knows how to put the right combination of players together to bring out the best in each one of them. He or she sees the skills and abilities of each player on the team and knows how to effectively put them together to bring about the best result. Sometimes a coach will play someone in a different position or spot on the field or court than that player is used to, because it works better for the system as a whole. Sometimes a coach will have to cut or trade players from the team, because the skillset, dynamic or attitude do not fit or are detrimental to the overall culture or success. God wants to do the same with us. With His eye upon us (Psalm 32:8) he is looking at the dynamic of His team and determining our best position on it and the best players to put around us. We will look at this in more detail in Chapter 6 when it comes to who we choose to be on our teams, but there are times when God has to cut or trade people away from our teams in order for us to grow or fulfill the call on our lives.

Let's look at it from the perspective of 1 Corinthians 12:4-27 (New International Version) where it says:

> There are different kinds of gifts (skills or abilities), but the same Spirit distributes them. There are different kinds of service, but the same Lord (Coach). There are different kinds of working (player positions), but in all of them and in everyone it is the same God (Coach) at work.

> Now to each one the manifestation of the Spirit is given for the common good. To one there is given through the Spirit a message of wisdom, to another a message of knowledge by means of the same Spirit, to another faith by the same Spirit, to another gifts of healing by that one Spirit, to another miraculous powers, to another distinguishing between spirits, to another speaking in different kinds of tongues, and to still another the interpretation of tongues. All these are the work of one and the same Spirit, and he distributes them to each one, just as he determines.

> Just as a body (team), though one, has many parts (players), but all its many parts (players) form one body (team), so it is with Christ. For we were all baptized by one Spirit so as to form one body (team)- whether Jews or Gentiles, slave or free- and we were all given the one Spirit to drink. Even so the body (team) is not made up of one part (player) but of many.

> Now if the foot should say, "Because I am not a hand, I do not belong to the body," it would not for that reason stop being part of the body. And if the ear should say, "Because I am not an eye, I do not belong to the body," it would not for that reason stop being part of the body. If the whole body were an eye, where would the sense of hearing be? If the whole body were an ear, where would the sense of smell be? But in fact God has placed the parts in the body, every one of them, just as he wanted them to be. If they were all one part, where would the body be? As it is there are many parts, but one body.

> The eye cannot say to the hand, "I don't need you!" And the head cannot say to the feet, "I don't need you!" On the contrary, those parts of the body that seem to weaker are indispensable, and the parts that we think are less honorable we treat with special honor. And the parts that are unpresentable are treated with special modesty, while our presentable parts need no special treatment. But God has put the body (team) together, giving greater honor to the parts (players) that lacked it, so that there should be no

division in the body (team), but that its parts (players) should have equal concern for each other. If one part (player) suffers, every part (player) suffers with it; if one part (player) is honored, every part (player) rejoices with it.

Now you are the body (team) of Christ, and each one of you is a part (player) of it.

If you go back through that section of scripture and read it again, this time substituting the words that are in parentheses, it will hopefully take on a bit of a different meaning for you from God's perspective. We are the players on His team. He positions us where He needs us to be on His team and puts the right combination of players around for us to be our most effective. In my own time as a coach I can relate to this idea. In practices I have to be cognizant of the players who are distracting to one another and structure drills in a way that they are working with other teammates that help them focus and train. In games I need to structure my players on the field in the positions that best suit their skill set as well as putting the right players around one another in order to complement each other. Certain players work better with one another, and others don't mix as well.

God is looking at this process on a much larger scale, but He is also concerned about it when it comes to you and me individually. If we look back at 1 Corinthians 12:18 (New International Version) it says "But God has placed the parts in the body, *every one of them*, just as he wanted them to be." He has a plan for how He wants His team to be structured and where we individually fit. He also has a plan for the parts He wants around us. Sometimes there are changes I need to make as a coach when I evaluate my players and the team chemistry. God is no different in my life and yours. As He is coaching us He will at times have to steer us away from toxic relationships or *players* that are distracting us or not pushing us to be our best. This can be difficult and lonely at times for all of us, but there is a plan.

God, like a good coach, wants to give us clear direction for our lives. Am I seeking Him, listening and obeying His direction? I can attest that He has been faithful in my life as He has guided me to grow as a man. I can also attest that there have been definite times where it has not been easy to obey. God has closed some doors on relationships and opportunities in my own life that I still don't understand. He has also opened doors with my career where the job I think is best for my situation and finances is not the one I get. I've also known clearly when I seek Him which job He wants me to take and when to move on and when to stay put. Sometimes He tells me to stay put for a lot longer than I want to. Sometimes I am called to forgive offenses and forgive debts that don't seem fair to me. I have also been very blessed, and God has interceded on my behalf, protected and advocated for me on many occasions.

With that in mind do I trust Him and accept His teaching, rebuking, correcting and training in order to become the player He needs me to be?

Chapter 5

<u>What Is a Good Player?</u>

"I'll do whatever it takes to win games, whether it's sitting on a bench
waving a towel, handing a cup of water to a teammate, or hitting the
game-winning shot."

-Kobe Bryant

If you were to brainstorm the qualities of a good player or a good
teammate, here are some of the attributes that might come to my mind:
disciplined, dependable, coachable, confident, humble, prepared for the
game, productive on the field, puts in the extra work when no one is
watching, leads by example, listens to the coach, makes the players
around them better, doesn't play down to the level of the competition,
strives for excellence, stays on assignment, works on weaknesses, unifies
the team, opponents have to plan for them, and so on. This is obviously
not an exhaustive list, and I'm sure a few more things come to your mind
as you read this. However in this next chapter let's unpack some of these
attributes and ask ourselves if we are living these characteristics out
today.

Prepared for the Game and Productive on the Field

I realize these are two different attributes of a good player, but I
wanted to put them together for a reason. I was reading my Bible the
other morning and in Matthew 25:1-30 Jesus tells two parables or stories
back to back which I think illustrate these player attributes quite well:
The Parable of the Ten Bridesmaids and The Parable of the Three
Servants.

If you have ever read that section of scripture, then you may be
familiar with those parables. If not, I'll give you a quick synopsis. In The
Parable of the Ten Bridesmaids Jesus (Matthew 25:1-13) is comparing
the Kingdom of Heaven to 10 bridesmaids who are waiting for the
bridegroom to come. This story has some historical context rooted in the
Jewish stages of marriage back in Jesus' time. Marriages were arranged
by the families back then. There was a time of engagement and betrothal
and after about a year the bridegroom would come at an unexpected time
for his bride. The bridesmaids in this story all have lamps, so they can
see where they're going on their way to meet the bridegroom if he
happens to show up at night. Five of the bridesmaids bring extra oil for
their lamps (prepared) and five of the bridesmaids do not bring extra oil
(unprepared). The bridegroom is delayed, and the bridesmaids fall asleep

while waiting. At midnight the bridesmaids are awoken by shouts that the bridegroom is coming, and they go out to meet him. Since the bridegroom was delayed the lamps have run out of oil. The *prepared* bridesmaids have extra oil, and the *unprepared* ones ask them if they could give them some oil. Their response is that there isn't enough oil to spare, but they could run to a shop and buy some. While those five unprepared bridesmaids are out shopping for oil, the five prepared ones meet the bridegroom and go into the wedding feast, and the door to the feast is locked. The five unprepared bridesmaids come back, but by this time it is too late.

Next The Parable of the Three Servants (Matthew 25:14-30) is about a master who has to go away on a long trip. He has three servants and gives them some money according to their abilities before he leaves. To one servant he gives five bags of silver. To another he gives two bags. And to the third he gives one bag. While he is gone the first two servants get to work investing and growing the master's money. The third servant however took the money and buried it in a hole. When the master returned from the trip he was very pleased with the first two servants who doubled his money but was quite angry with the third servant who did nothing (unproductive). He calls the last servant lazy and tells him he could've at least put the money in the bank where it would have earned some interest. The master then takes that servant's one bag of silver and gives it to the one with ten bags (productive) and tosses the unproductive servant out.

How do these stories relate to the attributes of being a good player? I'll make the connection for you by telling you a quick story of my own. I coached a kid for a couple of seasons who was a pretty talented soccer player. He enjoyed playing for me, but I knew he needed to be playing at a higher level of competition in order to advance in the sport. I spoke with his dad about it after the second season of him playing for me and encouraged him to find a club team where his son could be pushed to grow in his game. He tried out and got onto a team, but it was apparent from the beginning that he was not going to be a starter for this team right away. He would have to earn his stripes so to speak. He showed up to practices and worked, but during his first season with this new team he did not get a lot of game time. The most time he would get was about half a game, but most of the time it was less than that.

This was frustrating for him and his dad. The dad later asked me what his son needed to do to get more playing time and to eventually land a starting spot on the team. I sat down with both of them and asked the kid how much time he was putting in each day in working on his skills outside of scheduled practices, so he would be *prepared* for when his coach put him in during a game. The second thing I talked about with him was that he needed to be *productive* when he was given the chance to be on the field. He needed to make that time count. Create a play. Get an assist. Score a goal. Shut down the other team's players defensively. Do something that catches his coach's attention. Eventually he earned a starting spot on the team, but it only came after he was *prepared* and *productive*. The *unprepared* and *unproductive* people in the stories Jesus told didn't make the cut.

So looking at that I have to ask myself, am I that kind of player on God's team? Am I prepared when I'm called on by the Coach to go out on the field and make a difference in the game? Am I productive with my life and the opportunities that are given to me to love and serve others?

Strives for Excellence

Being a good player does not mean that you are the best on your team, but it does mean that you are pushing yourself to be the best you can be. Let's face it not all of us can or could have been the best player on the teams we were a part of. The truth of it is though often times those teams who have all the *best* players fall short for a number of reasons. A team needs role players and people who know their job and do it well.

As Christians on our fields of life now, we need to recognize the world needs the same thing. I have been told at times in my life that I am uneducated and foolish for what I believe. I don't try and argue this with those who have said such things. That is their perspective. I know for myself how important my faith has been to me and how it directs my life on a daily basis. I respect them and their story. However what I do think is undeniable and beyond argument is a Christian who strives for excellence. Am I an excellent husband, father, employee, neighbor, friend, volunteer? Am I the kind of person you want on your team? That is where our real influence lies. If I strive for excellence in all I do and go above and beyond to make the world and the community around me a better place for everyone, it's hard to argue with that.

I have also managed people in various work settings through the years who say they are Christians but turn out to be not very good employees. I had to supervise them pretty closely to make sure they were doing their job, and they were pretty difficult for other staff to get along with. That is an issue that should never be the case and those people's poor work ethic greatly diminishes their testimony. Conversely players who strive for excellence are ones that everyone wants on their team.

To illustrate this point I want to tell a story about my wife Jaime. She is a lady who wears a lot of hats. One of those hats is a real estate agent. Jaime started in that business some years back and hit the ground running as she does in almost everything. She strives to be the best at whatever she does. She is the kind of person who sees an issue and jumps in with both feet to make it better. She was very productive within her first year at the job finishing second in sales amongst all of the real estate agents in our town. This caught the eye of many of the real estate brokers, and she was approached to join the top agency in our area. A year or so later she did accept an offer to work there and within six months of working this new job she was in the top seven of the 60 agents in that office. Because my wife was striving for excellence in her work, on her *field*, she got a seat at the table of that real estate office, however the story doesn't end there.

Getting an invite to work at her new office didn't mean her work was over. She couldn't "rest on her laurels" as the saying goes. If she did sit back and coast at her new job I don't think the following story would have happened. Her work ethic became her witness for Jesus to that new office. In Proverbs 22:29 (New King James Version) it says "Do you see a man who excels in his work? He will stand before kings." One day her new boss spent some time talking with Jaime because of the relationship that was built due to her professional acumen. She had proved herself to be a valuable player, and Jaime shared an Andy Stanley podcast with him on the topic of success (To those of you who don't know who Andy Stanley is, he is an author and senior pastor of North Point Community Church in the Atlanta area). Her boss enjoyed it and then shared it at their weekly staff meeting. He also went on to tell my wife that he had been listening to numerous sermons since. Striving for excellence didn't just get Jaime a seat at the table, it also gave her a voice at the table. It gave her an opportunity to share the gospel message with some people that may never go to church, and it wouldn't have happened if she wasn't given the platform afforded to her from excelling in her work.

There are some examples of stories of people in the Bible that illustrate this concept as well. Let's look specifically at the life of Daniel. You can read the whole story in the book of Daniel, but I'll give you a quick snapshot. At that time in history, Jerusalem was besieged and conquered by Babylon. The king of Babylon, Nebuchadnezzar, then picked out some of the children of Israel to train and groom to be servants in his palace. Of those that were chosen four young men from the tribe of Judah stood out. These young men committed themselves to not be defiled by Nebuchadnezzar's food or the culture that surrounded them. They stayed true to God, and He blessed them for it. When Nebuchadnezzar interviews the four of them "he found them ten times better than all of the magicians and enchanters that were in all his kingdom (Daniel 1:20 English Standard Version)." Ten times better! Their commitment to God and excellence in their lives earned them a seat at the king's table and their ongoing faith in God to the point of obedience even when their lives were threatened ensured protection and freedom of worship for all of Israel.

Players who pushed themselves to be the best they could be would get the attention and respect of both the coach and the team. It would also often give them an audience with the coach and a voice on how things are going on the team.

How are we pushing ourselves towards excellence today? Does our work ethic and character give us influence in our families, work and communities? Are we using that influence to love and serve others as Jesus would?

Doesn't Play to the Level of the Competition

For any of us who have been around athletics or watched sports we've heard this statement from a coach or commentator stating "Play your game. Don't play to the level of your competition." As most of you probably already know when a team or player plays to the level of their competition, they are motivated and ready when it comes to playing against a really good team and then play less than their potential when facing an easier opponent. In short they're inconsistent. This was the topic of my end of the season speech to my team in the fall of 2019. They were a team who played to the level of their competition, much to my frustration throughout the season. It's very hard as a coach to see the level a team can play at and the potential they have when they play really well against good competition, only to lose games against teams they should beat.

Good players bring their "A game" regardless of their opponent. They are consistent game in and game out. As a coach and a teammate you know what to expect when that player steps on the field or on the court. They lead others by their example of consistency.

Can people say the same about me? Do I bring my best to every area of life or do I only do that with people I want to impress? Do I treat people equally? Am I the same at work as I am at home or do I just work hard and have nothing left for my family? Am I the same player when I have a winning season as well as a losing season? Am I the same player even when the rest of my team, friends or family are inconsistent?

It's amazing to see what God can do with consistent people. Note I didn't say perfect people. I said consistent people. God described King David as a man after His own heart (Acts 13:22). God makes a covenant with David that his kingdom and throne shall be established forever (2 Samuel 7:16). Why does God do this? What was it about David? If you know anything about David's story, then you know when he sinned, he sinned big. He raped another man's wife, got her pregnant and then had her husband killed to cover it up. That doesn't strike me as a guy I would go to for spiritual advice or life coaching. When he is confronted by the prophet Nathan in 2 Samuel 12, he repents and fasts. He returns to God. He doesn't try to keep running away and do things his way.

In fact throughout his life David was consistent in returning to the wisdom of God. He was consistent as a shepherd taking care of his father's sheep when no one knew who he was. He was consistent in his belief in God when he faced giants (bears, lions and Goliath) in his life. He was consistent when he was being persecuted and running for his life from King Saul and stayed consistent as the king of Israel for 40 years. David is in the lineage of Jesus. He was not perfect, but God did amazing things through his life and the generations after him, because he stayed true and consistent in his walk with God.

Elevates Everyone's Game

Have you ever played on a team or with a player where you wanted to play better? You knew you had to play your best because of that player. A good player unifies a team and elevates everyone's game. Those players set the tone and example for their team by their work ethic and their leadership. To start this chapter I quoted a man who embodied those two things in the world of basketball, Kobe Bryant. The interesting thing is that I began writing this chapter before the tragic death of him and his daughter on January 26, 2020, so his story and that quote resonates even more now. I went to high school in southeast Pennsylvania, and my school played against Lower Merion, where Kobe played high school ball. In high school it was very apparent he was something special. He was leaps ahead of the rest of the players in that class, and there were actually a few other guys that went on to play in the NBA that came out of that area from that high school class.

There are many stories about him and his work ethic, but I want to highlight a few examples. In high school (yes high school) he would show up and practice from 5am-7am and stay after practice and play one-on-one games to 100 points. When he was 18 years old and playing for the Lakers he would show up two hours before practice and shoot baskets in a dark gym. Kobe was the first player to come to practice, even when he was hurt. He would watch film of himself at halftime of a game to analyze where he could improve. And the list goes on and on. His basketball accomplishments include: 1996 Pennsylvania State Basketball Champions, five time NBA champion, 17 time NBA All-Star, 1997 Slam Dunk Champion, 12 all-defensive team selections, most three pointers made in a game (12), two time NBA Finals MVP, and two Olympic gold medals.

There are varying opinions out there from former teammates as to what it was like playing with Kobe, but I think it would go without saying that if you played alongside him you wanted to bring your best game to the court.

Am I that type of player? Does my work ethic and leadership elevate others in my life today to be at their best?

Puts in the Extra Work When No One is Watching

I don't know if it's just me, but I'm guessing I'm not alone in this. My question is "Do your kids get really frustrated in sports when they try something new and they can't do it right away?" I know my kids will probably get a little angry with me for writing this, but it's true. And this won't be the first time they've heard this from me. What I noticed from them, and also a number of other kids I've coached over the years to be fair, is that they honestly think they should get a certain skill down without having to work for it. That skill could be anything: shooting a basket, dribbling or throwing a ball, passing or shooting a soccer ball, etc. I don't recall if I acted the same way when I was young. I imagine I probably did. In any case, as a coach and as a father, I talk to my kids and my players about how if they want to get good at anything in life, athletics or not, they have to put in the work when no one is watching. They have to practice when they're not at practice!

In 2017 the band Twenty One Pilots won the Grammy Award for Best Pop Duo/Group Performance for their song Stressed Out. In a video interview with Alternative Press called "Shooting Hoops with Twenty One Pilots" lead singer Tyler Joseph discusses how his mom used to make him shoot 500 baskets every day before he could come in for dinner. The hope was that he would get good enough at basketball to earn a college scholarship. He eventually did get that scholarship but turned it down to pursue his career in music, and the rest is history (Whitt, 2013). He doesn't openly acknowledge it in the interview, but it isn't a big stretch to see that the discipline and practice that Tyler put into his basketball game every day translated to his music endeavors.

Another example of this I remember was from reading a book as a kid about Herschel Walker. For those of you who don't know who I'm talking about, he was a running back in the NFL from 1986-1997. He won the Heisman Trophy in 1982 and was selected twice for the Pro Bowl in 1987 and 1988. I honestly can't remember the name of the book, but I remember being amazed at his workout regimen as a kid in high school. In an article I read about him called "The Herschel Walker Workout" the authors discussed how he was overweight as a kid and had a speech impediment. He was picked on and bullied in elementary and middle school. In 1989 he wrote a book with Terry Todd, PhD entitled *Basic Training*. In the book Walker recalls approaching a track coach after his 6th grade year who worked with his older siblings and telling him how he wanted to get stronger and faster. The coach told Walker to do push-ups, sit-ups and sprints. Walker recalls "That's all he said. But it was enough." Walker is 59 years old and has been daily doing 2000-3000 push-ups and sit-ups ever since. He didn't even start playing organized sports until 7th grade and didn't play football until 9th grade, but he stayed true to his workout. I think this quote from him in the article captures it well:

> "What a good feeling that was too, to know all that hard work was paying off, and to know that even though I wasn't all that good to begin with, I could get better. I remember a bunch of kids I grew up with who had a heap more talent than I had but who never trained much or tried very hard. I'm not saying they didn't try at games, but almost anybody'll try hard in a real game. What matters is how hard you try before the game, especially when nobody is watching you. That's what's important. If you can bear down and really train and try hard before the game, the game'll take care of itself (McKay & McKay, 2016)."

What am I doing in my life now "when nobody is watching?" Am I putting in the extra work? How am I living my life each day to be prepared so that "the game'll take care of itself?"

Stays on Assignment

For those of you who have ever coached young kids or watched a game with young kids it sometimes looks like a swarm of bees running around a field after the ball. As those players progress through the years the hope is that they start to learn different formations and positions and begin to play accordingly. It's cute when kids are young and play like that. It's frustrating and counterproductive if a player still operates in that fashion after he or she has been around the game for a while. We've all seen it, and I have definitely coached some of those kids who run all over the field and are constantly out of position, leaving the team vulnerable. Those types of players have an issue with understanding their roles within the team structure and trusting their teammates. They have an issue with staying on their assignment. If I were to be honest with myself, often in life I can be one of those kids.

We understand in athletics why the player's positions and coach's assignments are important. Nothing effective would be accomplished as a team if everyone just played wherever they wanted and did whatever they wanted to do. The coach gives out specific assignments to each player in order to give the team the best chance at success. Good players understand this. God does the same with you and me today. I'll be honest here for a bit and tell you that I on occasion, well probably more than that, will gripe and complain about the assignment God gives me. I'll tell Him in no uncertain terms that I want a different job or a different living situation would be better for me or I want those friendships or that car or that house or whatever else comes spewing out of my mouth when I am not happy with my assignment. I have a choice to listen and follow through or run all over the field accomplishing nothing.

I'm going to take a detour from sports stories and talk about the life of Mother Teresa to illustrate this point. She is a celebrated figure in the world and in the Catholic Church due to her lifetime of work for the poor and sick in India. She dedicated her life at age 18 to the church and began teaching with the Loreto Sisters in Ireland. She was then posted to a school in India where she served for the next 20 years. Seeing the poverty around her she had what she describes as "a call within a call." God was directing her to a new assignment away from teaching and to caring for the poor. She describes it this way:

> Our Lord wants me to be a free nun covered with the poverty of the cross. Today, I learned a good lesson. The poverty of the poor must be so hard for them. While looking for a home I walked and walked till my arms and legs ached. I thought how much they must ache in body and soul, looking for a home, food and health. Then, the comfort of Loreto came to tempt me. "You only have to say the word and that will be yours again," The Tempter kept on saying…Of free choice my God, and out of love for you, I desire to remain and do whatever be your Holy will in my regard. I did not let a single tear come (Spink, 1997, p. 37).

Mother Teresa had already given up so much just by committing her life to the church, however God had another position He needed her to play. You can read it in the quote above how she struggled with her new assignment and wanted to return to the comforts of her former convent. Just imagine all of the lives that she never would have helped if she did go back and didn't stay on her assignment.

What about Jesus? What if Jesus didn't stay on His assignment? His assignment while He was here is simply stated in John 6:38 (Holman Christian Standard Bible) where He says "For I have come down from heaven, not to do My will, but the will of Him who sent Me." God's will for Jesus while on earth was to love and heal others and ultimately lay down His life (John 10:17-18) for us. The reality of this hits Him the night before He is to be betrayed and crucified where he cries out to God in prayer in Luke 22:42 (New Living Translation) saying "Father, if you are willing, please take this cup of suffering away from me. Yet I want your will to be done, not mine." Jesus experienced all of the same emotions as we do and knew the suffering He was going to face. Just imagine if He didn't stay on His assignment.

What about us? What about you? What about me? How would my life be different if I stayed on my assignment from God? How would my marriage, family, work, community and church be different?

Societally it's a pretty safe bet that if we were to do that our divorce rates and numbers of fatherless homes would decrease. Our communities and jobs might improve as we took more ownership of where we lived and worked. Not following the assignment given by the coach when we played in the game caused chaos and confusion on the field. Jesus warns us of this and the importance of staying with our assignment when He says in Matthew 7:13-14 (New International Version) "Enter by the narrow gate, for wide is the gate and broad is the way that leads to destruction, and there are many who go in by it. Because narrow is the gate and difficult is the way which leads to life, and there are few who find it." God wants to help us to "enter by the narrow gate" and find "life," but we have to stick it out with Him even when the way gets "difficult."

Unifies the Team

Good players, and in fact good leaders, are very cognizant of the words that come out of their mouths. They realize that words matter. They understand the power of the tongue (Proverbs 18:21). It is sometimes unsalvageable as a coach when a team begins to tear itself down, and most of the time that happens by the way that the team speaks to one another. The trash talk, back biting, infighting and negativity towards each other can have irreparable effects upon the chemistry of a team and an individual player's psyche. Good coaches know they need to address those issues immediately and not let them fester. Good players know they need to speak positivity and encouragement to their teammates. Good players build relationships and speak life to their teammates. Good players unify their teams. They do this through their speech and more importantly their actions.

In James 3:3-6, 13-18 (The Message) it says:

A bit in the mouth of a horse controls the whole horse. A small rudder on a huge ship in the hands of a skilled captain sets a course in the face of the strongest winds. A word out of your mouth may seem of no account, but it can accomplish nearly anything- or destroy it!

It only takes a spark, remember, to set off a forest fire. A careless or wrongly placed word out of your mouth can do that. By our speech we can ruin the world, turn harmony into chaos, throw mud on a reputation, send the whole world up in smoke and go up in smoke with it, smoke right from the pit of hell.

Do you want to be counted as wise, to build a reputation for wisdom? Here's what you do: Live well, live wisely, live humbly. It's the way you live, not the way you talk that counts. Mean-spirited ambition isn't wisdom. Twisting the truth to make yourselves sound wise isn't wisdom. It's the furthest thing from wisdom- it's animal cunning, devilish plotting. Whenever you're trying to look better than others or get the better of others, things fall apart and everyone ends up at the others' throats.

Real wisdom, God's wisdom, begins with a holy life and is characterized by getting along with others. It is gentle and reasonable, overflowing with mercy and blessings, not hot one day and cold the next, not two-faced. You can develop a healthy, robust community that lives right with God and enjoys its results *only* if you do the hard work of getting along with each other, treating each other with dignity and honor.

These verses are pretty clear in terms of God's desire for us to speak and live lives which unify the teams around us. Negative and divisive language and behavior can be like a cancer in a locker room. Some of you may have played on teams where you experienced this, and I'm sure most of us have seen professional sports teams where management has had to clean house, players and coaches, in order to rectify these types of situations.

So do the words of my mouth accomplish or destroy? Does my speech ruin the world around me or turn harmony into chaos? Am I living wisely and humbly or with mean-spirited ambition? Am I trying to get the better of others or am I gentle and reasonable and putting in the hard work of getting along with others?

Opponents Have to Plan How to Stop Them

An opposing team has to strategize how they will defend or stop a good player. They don't really need to worry or plan too much for a nominal or mediocre player. That is not to say there isn't some strategy put in place for those players, however when a coach is scouting another team or is discussing game plans with another coach, statements such as "Watch out for #8" or "You'll need to put your best defender on #16" or something to that effect are often said. In order to win or have success against another team, a coach needs to plan on how to neutralize the other team's best players.

You're probably thinking to yourself "Okay, so what? That's pretty obvious. Nothing earth shattering in that concept." I agree, but if you look at it through a spiritual lens it starts to come into focus for how it applies to our lives now. A lot of times in life I find myself asking

"Why am I going through this struggle right now? I just wish it would go away." We've discussed already how God pushes us to our potential, and how trials just like training help us to get there. What we haven't quite looked at is the other side of the coin in which the adversary, the devil, is trying to take us out of the game. He does this through our marriages, our children, our finances, our health, etc.

I think there are two types of suffering found in scripture. One kind is the type we deserve, because we did something wrong. It is a consequence for our poor choices or actions. The other kind is suffering for doing the right thing. This is outlined pretty well in the following passage in 1 Peter 2:18-20 (The Message):

> You who are servants, be good servants to your masters- not just to good masters, but also to bad ones. What counts is that you put up with it for God's sake when you're treated badly for no good reason. There's no particular virtue in accepting punishment that you well deserve. But if you're treated badly for good behavior and continue in spite of it to be a good servant, that is what counts with God.

A man who was well acquainted with suffering for doing the right thing was the Apostle Paul. He wrote in 2 Corinthians 4:8-10 (New King James Version) "We are hard-pressed on every side, yet not crushed: we are perplexed, but not in despair; persecuted, but not forsaken; struck down, but not destroyed- always carrying about in the body the dying of the Lord Jesus, that the life of Jesus also may be manifested in our body."

Jesus, who was beaten and crucified for no wrongdoing of His own, says in John 16:33 (English Standard Version) "I have said these things to you, that in Me you may have peace. In the world you will have tribulation. But take heart, because I have overcome the world."

Throughout the Bible there is story after story of people who have had to struggle for doing the right thing. Further along in 2 Corinthians 4:17-18 (New King James Version) Paul writes "For our light affliction, which is but for a moment, is working for us a far more exceeding and eternal weight of glory, while we do not look at the things which are seen, but at the things which are not seen. For the things which are seen are temporary, but the things which are not seen are eternal."

If you're going through struggles in life for doing the right thing, then you're in good company. The devil is scheming ways to try to stop you, to get you off God's game plan. The other side of that coin is asking yourself why you're *not* going through trials.

Am I seeking comfort? Am I settling in life for a nominal role on God's team? Does the devil have to strategize how to defend me or do I pose no real threat to him with how I live my life?

Works On Weaknesses

Most of us are born either being right-handed or left-handed. We have a dominant side that we use to write, throw, kick, etc. There are a minority of people who are ambidextrous, but the majority of us use one side of our body over the other. In the world of athletics as we grow older and start to progress in a given sport that we enjoy, this one-sided aspect of our skill development becomes an issue. This was especially noticeable for me when I coached soccer and basketball. Players would only focus on the dominant side of their body when practicing their skills. When I asked them to do the same thing with their other hand or foot, they seemed lost. Players were mystified that they couldn't execute the same skill with the opposite side of their body. I would explain to them that the mechanics for that given skill were the same, but they would need to put in extra practice in order to get that side of their body up to speed. I explained to them that until they were able to become proficient with both sides of their body they would always be easy to defend. They had a glaring weakness, because they could only effectively go one way with their game. I recall going through this period of my development in those sports and forcing myself to focus on the left side of my body to develop that hand and foot. It was awkward at times, and it would feel like I was taking a step back in my game as well, but it was essential for me to go through it to get better.

Good players are not satisfied in what they already do well, but they push themselves to work on the weaknesses in their game.

This mindset is captured in a statement made by Chelsea Football Club defender Antonio Rudiger when he said:

> "From every coach, you want him to improve you. I don't want to hear what I'm doing good. I want to hear what I'm not doing good and what I can improve. This is what I want to see from him (Chelsea defender Antonio Rudiger reveals the tactical difference between Thomas Tuchel and Frank Lampard, 2021)."

Every one of us has things we are good at and things we can improve upon. We can either address the areas of our lives that need improvement and growth or we can ignore them. If we didn't address the weaknesses in our game as athletes we didn't progress. The same is true now. I am not going to be good at everything, but when I know God is pushing me to grow in a certain area of my life it behooves me to listen and do something about it. It will take extra work just like it did when we

71

had to learn to use our opposite hand or foot. It will be uncomfortable and awkward, but He is with us and wants to help us in our weaknesses.

In 2 Corinthians 12:9 (English Standard Version) Paul writes:

But he said to me, "My grace is sufficient for you, for my power is made perfect in weakness." Therefore I will boast all the more gladly of my weaknesses, so that the power of Christ may rest upon me.

So am I the kind of player who only wants "to hear what I'm doing good?" Or am I the kind of player who wants to improve and grow to be the best I can?

PART 3
(WHO)

Chapter 6

<u>Who Is On Your Team?</u>

"You are the average of the five people you spend most of your time with."

-Jim Rohn

I have often talked with patients and my own children about how important and influential their friends are. The truth is parents that the older your children get the less influence you will have. Our peers become the most influential factor in our lives. Before we get all worked up about this as parents, understand this is a good thing. We want our influence on our children to become less, so that they grow up and branch out and leave the nest so to speak. This statement however should be a wake-up call that we only have a limited amount of time as parents in which our parenting is truly influential upon our kids. We need to use that time wisely. The real issue is if our children remain dependent on us, then we have not done a very good job as parents preparing our children for life. A big part of that job is helping our kids to analyze their friendships and understand its impact upon their lives.

In order to drive this point home ask yourself a few questions:

1. Who were my friends back in high school and/or college?
2. What are they doing professionally and personally in their lives now?
3. What am I doing professionally or personally in my life now?

In most cases there is a pretty good connection, and obviously there are exceptions, between who your friends were, what they're doing now and what you're doing now. That is the unrealized influence of the "team" that you put around yourself in those formative years. That's also the influence of the people you put around yourself now. That's the reason your parents asked or should have asked you who your friends were and got to know those who were influencing their children's future. In Proverbs 13:20 (New King James Version) it says "He who walks with wise men will be wise, But the companion of fools will be destroyed." Today as parents we have to take it a step further than our parents did and investigate not only our children's friends but also who is influencing them online as well.

When we were kids and it came to athletics or competition it was a little more cut and dry. Sure if we were the captain of the team for a pick-up game of basketball or football we might pick our best friend, but most of the time we would pick the best players. We did this because we wanted to have the best team, the winning team.

So the question is "Who are we picking to be on our team today?" A follow up thought to that is for us to look at the team we've picked and process what kind of influence they have on us. Is it good? Is it pushing us or challenging us to grow? Do the members of our team listen to and encourage us? Do they hold us accountable?

The Importance of a Good Team

I have played on a number of different teams throughout my life, and I understood the importance of a good team. However after college and my athletic career ceased I sort of lost touch with the team concept. I got married and moved west, leaving my support system of friends and family that I knew. My wife and I became a team, but it's never healthy to have only one person be your support system. I needed to rebuild my team. I needed teammates. So what do I mean by a "teammate?" One of my professors in graduate school, Dr. Gary Collins, told us in class once that as therapists we are going to need people in our lives that we can show the good, bad and ugly sides of ourselves to in order to do this work. I've been in this profession for over 20 years now and can definitely see the wisdom of his statement, and I also think that is what we need from the people we choose to be on our team.

This became very clear to me after the birth of my first child. I had a full-time job and a couple of part-time jobs as I was working on completing my hours towards licensure as a psychotherapist. This meant a lot of late nights and long hours. On top of that process, Jaime and I were living in a two bedroom house at the time and were discussing if it was going to be big enough for our growing family. After praying about it and analyzing the housing market in California at the time, it made sense for us to build on to our house as opposed to moving into a different place.

We hired an architect who gave us an estimate on how much it would cost for us to build the addition, and took out the money from the equity of our home. After getting approved for the money we began to search for contractors to do the work. Every contractor we contacted was either too busy to take the job or wanted significantly more money than we had to do the job. This put us in quite a bind, and we were up against the clock. It became clear that if we were going to get this addition built before Jaime gave birth we were going to need to do this on our own. I had some construction work experience from jobs I worked in between summers during college, but I wasn't a licensed contractor. I called a friend who had his contractor's license and laid out our situation to him. He graciously said he would help us out. We got our permit approved by the county and were able to break ground in early December, however Jaime's due date was in late February. We were planning on building two bedrooms off the back of the house and remodeling our kitchen.

Now when I say that we live in California, this is not the part of California most of you are thinking of. It's not palm trees and sun and sand. We live in a mountain town where we can sometimes get snow storms that dump up to five feet at a time, so breaking ground in December is not a very opportune time to build. Well that particular winter, the storms held off. The weather was cold, but we could build, and for the next few months that's what we did. I continued to work multiple jobs, and as soon as I got home I put my tool belt on and started building. That was our story for the next few months. I never took a day off and worked many days late into the night by spotlight. Even Jaime would be banging nails into the wee hours, baby bump and all. By the grace of God and the help of a lot of friends we were able to get the house completed to a place where it was livable. In fact it felt like an episode of one of those home makeover shows, since we were still coordinating things with the painters and flooring people while Jaime was in the hospital getting ready to give birth. Our friends were gracious enough to take care of some of the last details of the addition before we got back home from the hospital with our new *addition*.

Isaiah Jonathan Stiansen was born on February 22, 2006. There are a lot of emotions you experience as a new parent: joy, excitement, anxiety, fear, bewilderment, and exhaustion to name a few. The one feeling I didn't think I would experience was depression. In my line of work I obviously know about Postpartum Depression and have treated patients who experience it, however I have to admit I wasn't very aware that men can suffer from it as well, a condition known as Paternal Postpartum Depression (PPPD). Four years after the birth of my first kid in 2010 the *Journal of American Medical Association* published a study that showed about 10% of men suffer from depression after the birth of their child (Paulson & Bazemore, 2010, p. 1961). So come to find out later on I wasn't alone in this, but I definitely felt alone while I was going through it. I wasn't a stranger to depression. My dad and his mother suffered from it, and I had episodes with it in the past. When I look back I could see that I would go through depressive episodes around big events in my life (leading up to getting married, graduate school, and now the birth of my first child), however this time around the symptoms were a lot worse than they had ever been in the past.

If I were to be honest I would say that this depressive episode lasted close to 18 months. It was miserable, and I know it was difficult on my wife and family. I remember not being able to sleep or eat. I didn't want to talk to anyone. I remember going to work and praying to God that my voicemail and emails were empty, and that no one needed anything from me (which never happened). I felt awkward and foolish. I second guessed every decision and everything that came out of my mouth and felt like an idiot every time I talked with friends or family about what was going on with me. I felt like I repeated myself all the time, like a broken record, trying to make sense of why I was feeling this way. I was numb, sad, anxious and angry and felt like my head was in this constant fog that I couldn't shake. I met with a couple of therapists during this time and had some space to vent a bit. One of them told me one session that maybe I needed to see that nothing was really wrong in my life. I couldn't disagree with him on the surface, but I wished so badly that inside I could feel that way. I pressed on with work and trying to put the finishing touches on the house, but I never felt productive. I was just there, in body but not in spirit. I would have moments where the cloud lifted, and I felt like I could finally breathe and see the colors around me and feel the breeze on my face. However it would only last for 15 or 20 minutes, and the cloud would settle back on me. Those of you who are reading this and have ever struggled with depression can probably relate to what I was going through.

I was praying a lot through this time. Honestly I was praying mostly for God to just take this away from me. That didn't seem to happen. In fact it felt like it just kept going and going and there was never going to be an end. In my prayers and seeking however there were two things that got impressed upon my spirit. The first one was that I needed to set better boundaries in my life, and the second was that I needed to ask for help. I needed to let my yes be yes, and my no be no (Matthew 5:37). I also needed to be vulnerable to people, ask for help and build my support system. I needed to build my team.

In terms of boundaries, I have always been pretty good at setting boundaries with others, but I wasn't very good with setting boundaries for myself. I had this idea in my head that I could do anything I put my mind to. It's not a bad thought on the surface, but the issue in my heart was that most of the time it was done in my own strength and for my own glory. It was the "ego" temptation we looked at earlier in Chapter 3 when Jesus is being tempted by Satan. I wanted to prove I could do it even to the detriment of my mind, body and spirit. I had overloaded my system. I had tried to take on too much, and it broke me. It wasn't a fun lesson to learn but an essential one.

The second lesson was probably harder for me to learn. I'm not somebody that finds it easy to ask for help. I pride myself on being resourceful and determined. If there is a way to solve an issue, then I will find it. The problem here is that I couldn't find a way to solve this episode of depression. God was giving me direction and a game plan to follow to help me out of it, but I was resistant. He was telling me that I needed some men in my life that could see "the good, bad and ugly" sides of me, who would be an ear to listen and would pray for me. I didn't disagree with Him, but I wasn't too excited about the process of building that team.

I'm an introvert and being neck deep in depression didn't really help the situation very much in terms of reaching out to people to build a support system. I sought God in prayer about who He wanted me to reach out to, and He gave me a couple of names. These guys were already friends of mine and we held similar values and beliefs, so that helped. I called them both up and arranged a time when we could all meet. I honestly felt pretty silly opening up to them about the struggles I had been having. I judged myself as being irrational and overreacting about things. In any case I got through it and told them that I was going to need to get together a couple of times a month with them to just touch base with each other. I also asked if they would be open to me calling them between meetings to talk if needed. They were both cool with it. We prayed for each other and that was that. Our meetings progressed to become a time where each guy would share where he was at with his marriage, family, work and relationships. We eventually added another guy to the mix and the four of us met as regularly as we could for the next year or two.

We simply had a time where we could be open and talk about life and God and encourage each other. We were able to be real with one another about the sin and struggles in our lives and hold one another accountable to grow and get better. I am still good friends with a couple of those guys to this day. We don't meet as a group anymore, but we still get together from time to time and our families still spend time with one another. I can still share my heart and struggles and prayer requests with those guys to this day, and we began meeting over a decade ago. One of those guys went on to run his own men's small group in his church, and another guy now pastors his own church. Out of that hardship God challenged me to be vulnerable and build real fellowship in my life.

Building Your Team

So let's spend a little time talking about that process of building fellowship. Keeping in mind you can't choose your family, but you can choose your friends it is important to distinguish between levels of friendship and the levels of influence that people have on us. Jesus can give us some insight on this. He had his group of 12 disciples, but three of them were closer to Him. There are three times where Jesus pulls those guys aside from the rest of the disciples (Matthew 5, Matthew 17, and Matthew 26), and He specifically seeks their encouragement, prayer and support in Matthew 26 the night before He was to be crucified. The three guys didn't do such a great job of it, since they fell asleep on Him a few times, but the point is still valid. Those three guys were His team.

From this example let's distinguish three categories of relationships and their influence on our lives:

1. Acquaintances
2. Friends
3. Teammates

Many of us have a number of people in our lives we call "friends" which I would actually categorize as acquaintances. They could be coworkers or people we share hobbies or interests with or people we see at group functions, church, etc. These relationships could grow into friendships, but typically they aren't very deep relationships in the beginning. You talk on the surface about your hobbies, sports, work, the weather or your summer vacation plans. There is nothing wrong with these relationships. We all have them, but we need to be cognizant of the level of influence they have on us. If we are overly concerned with what our acquaintances think of us or how they view us and alter our beliefs and values because of it, then we need to take a pause and realign. Unfortunately this scenario happens more and more with the influence of social media in our lives.

From acquaintances grow friendships. At this point you get to know one another a bit more. You may start to have these people over to your house for dinner and get to know their history and views on life. You begin to share life together. Your kids play with one another. You might even vacation with one another. As a relationship goes from acquaintance to friend, these relationships will become more influential in your life. A friend's opinions and views will hold more weight in your life. It is from this position that you begin to analyze and choose which friends will become your teammates. Teammates are those friends who can see the good, bad and ugly of you, and those friends you can trust and who will hold you accountable.

So looking back at the quote at the beginning of this chapter where it said that we "are the average of the five people we spend the most time with" it is very important that we seek God in this decision process. Am I asking God who He wants me to put on my team? Do I talk to Him about my friends and those that influence my life? Are my friends heading in a direction that God wants me to go? What is the fruit of their life? How do they treat others? Does their life line up with God's purposes, loving Him and loving others (Mark 12:30-31)? Do they challenge me to grow in the wisdom of God? Proverbs 27:17 (Contemporary English Version) says "Just as iron sharpens iron, friends sharpen the minds of each other." Does my team do that for me and push me to "play" my best in life? Praying through the answers to these questions will help us determine what friends we put on our team.

Also let me be clear that I am not saying any of this for us to cast aside our acquaintances and other friendships. They are still important people in our lives, and God has them there for us to love and to be a blessing to them. Our influence in their lives should point them to Him. On the flip side, we do need to be aware if they are influencing us away from the things of God. This distinction should be made with prayerful consideration as to what God would have us do with these relationships. Too often I have witnessed Christians who have had friends or neighbors in their lives who have rejected the things of God, and those Christians have wiped their hands clean of those people. From my own life I have had friends and neighbors whom I have known for decades that initially wanted nothing to do with God but are now open to hearing about the things of God because of our relationship over the years. God has used my life, my marriage and my family as a way to draw them to Him. The fruit of God in our lives over the years of our relationship became our witness. Remember the words of Jesus in Matthew 5:14-16 (New International Version) where He says "You are the light of the world. A town built on a hill cannot be hidden. Neither do people light a lamp and put it under a bowl. Instead they put it on its stand, and it gives light to everyone in the house. In the same way, let your light shine before others, that they may see your good deeds and glorify your Father in heaven."

For the remainder of the chapter I want to address a few more categories of influential people on our teams:

1. Spouse

I can't stress enough the importance of this choice in our lives. It is the only relationship in the Bible where we leave our family and become one flesh with another person (Genesis 2:24). We don't do this with a friend, relative or coworker. As a therapist I talk to so many people who are struggling in their marriages and consequently how it affects every other area of their life. In therapy I often take them back to the time when they were dating their current spouse and have them analyze some of the issues they saw back then. I understand that when you're in love often the blinders go on, and you gloss over or make excuses for a lot of those things. What we need to keep in mind is that those issues don't go away and often they intensify when you are married and living together. I am not saying that you need to find the perfect person or relationship. That doesn't exist. What I am saying is that you need to know yourself, what you want, and what God wants for you and have the confidence to move on from something that is not right for you.

In this process something else I tell my patients is that sex clouds our vision when it comes to dating relationships. God's playbook is pretty clear that He designed sex for the marriage relationship. I know this one pretty well as I talked about earlier in the book and how I lost my focus and was trapped in this sin. Many of my patients agree when they look back on their relationships and how things changed for them mentally and emotionally while they were dating someone when they started having sex. They saw some of the issues pretty clearly beforehand, but those issues became less important once they became sexually involved.

Outside of one's decision to accept Jesus as their Lord and Savior, our choice of spouse is the next most important and influential decision that we will make. I don't say this to scare people into never getting married. I say this so that we seek God's wisdom in this decision. Are we praying and asking Him about our dating relationships? Are we listening and obeying if He says something that goes against how we feel? If we're already married and have children, are we praying for our children in this decision and for their future spouses? You may think all of this seems a bit over the top or extreme, but as a marriage and family therapist I sadly listen to a lot of heartbreaking stories related to struggling marriages. I think the contrast is pretty clearly outlined in the following verses from the book of Proverbs and stresses the importance of involving God in the process of this decision.

Would you want this?

Proverbs 31:10-12 (English Standard Version) says "An excellent wife who can find? She is far more precious than jewels. The heart of her husband trusts in her, and he will have no lack of gain. She does him good, and not harm, all the days of her life."

Or this?

Proverbs 21:19 (English Standard Version) says "It is better to live in a desert land than with a quarrelsome and fretful woman."

It's a pretty easy answer, and I understand that we are all works in progress. God is working in all of us if we allow Him to, however if we are in a dating relationship where we don't trust the other person and the relationship brings us harm and not good and is filled with quarrels and fretting, it would be a good idea for us to reevaluate what we're doing there. A spouse is a partner we are building a life with day in and day out, and that person's character and values are paramount.

Here are a few pointers from my own experience and listening to others' stories over the years in regards to the process of choosing a spouse:

1. **Experience each other**- I would say you should date for at least a year and get to know one another past the infatuation stage. Spending this time allows you to see this person's values and character. What is important to them? Do your values line up with theirs? What are their goals? Where do they want to go in life? Do they do what they say? How do they handle conflict and stress? How do they treat others? How do they treat you? Do they bring you harm or good? Is the relationship marked by quarrels and fretting? Do I feel like I need to fix or change this person (usually not a good sign)? On the flip side do you bring this person harm or good? Are you trustworthy in this relationship?

2. **Equally yoked**- The Bible warns us against us being "unequally yoked (2 Corinthians 6:14)" which means that if we are a Christian

we should be wary about marrying someone who is not. However the Bible does address this and what we are supposed to do if we are unequally yoked in marriage (1 Corinthians 7:12-14). I have worked with a number of couples who are in this situation, and it can be very challenging on both parties. It is not impossible, but I have often seen a difference inherent in the values and the epistemology (the study of the nature of knowledge) of each person which makes communication and resolving conflict difficult.

Something else to chew on in terms of being equally yoked is that we look for a spouse that is on our playing level. What do I mean by that? Well if we look at it through the lens of our time as athletes we wanted to play on a team with the best players in order to have the most success on the field. Wouldn't it make sense that we would do the same thing when it came to the process of choosing our spouse? This may sound harsh to some, but I have listened to so many stories through my career of people feeling like they are pulling their spouse along in this journey of marriage. What if we chose someone who pushes us to be better? Who challenges us to grow?

We often settle in our relationships due to our own insecurities. Your spouse will not complete you, contrary to what Hollywood tells you. Their track record on relationships is not very good if you read any headline on any given day. One person's 50 percent is not completed by someone else's 50 percent. Could you imagine that thought process on any sports team you played on? Could you imagine saying to your teammate "Hey if I give 50% in the game today and you give 50%, then I think we might be okay out there?" There has never been a locker room pep talk in which a coach tells his players to go out there and give 50 percent. In order to be successful we have to give 100 percent of ourselves. Too often people who have not addressed their personal issues or shortcomings try to find someone else who also has not addressed their brokenness, and they magically expect success. Again I am not saying you have to be perfect or find the perfect partner. What I am saying is if you have an area of your life you need to work on or grow in, then pray about it and get to work. A dating relationship or marriage will not solve that area of your life for you. Put in the work and yoke yourself with someone who is willing to do the same.

3. **Enjoy each other**- All I want to say here is that life and marriage are hard enough as it is, so in looking for a spouse I recommend finding someone you enjoy. Do you have fun and laugh together? The Bible says it's good medicine (Proverbs 17:22). Do you have similar interests and hobbies or things that you enjoy doing together? I wouldn't say this is a deal breaker, but I would say it definitely helps. You don't have to like all of the same things but some

common interests go a long way. I have known some committed and good marriages that struggle simply because they have difficulty in this area. There are always going to be responsibilities and obligations along the journey of marriage (jobs, bills, kids, etc.), but at the end of it all you will be back with that person you married, just the two of you. God tells us in Proverbs 5:18 (Good News Translation) "So be happy with your wife and find your joy with the woman you married."

4. **Extended family**- This is an area that I didn't really think about much until I heard a number of stories and issues in this regard being addressed over my years as a therapist. It's not something that I remember being discussed when I went through pre-marital counseling either. What I am talking about here is that when you marry someone you also marry their family, so get to know them. I have been lucky to have some amazing in-laws. Every family has their issues, and we have had some of ours through the years, but I am fortunate. In my job I have listened to some terrible situations. This also isn't a deal breaker in my opinion, but it is something that will be a factor.

My Marriage Story

Even after seeking God for wisdom in this decision, all of us who are married know that it can be the greatest relationship of your life but will also take the most work of any relationship of your life. For perspective from my story, I got married when I was 23 years old. We got some feedback back then that we were too young to make that decision. In this day and age I know we would have definitely gotten the same advice. To this day I don't regret the decision a bit, but I have heard from a number of people who look at those who are happily married and think they have no problems or just got lucky. Anyone who has been at this marriage game for long knows that is not the truth.

Jaime and I dated in college, and we dated for three years before getting married. I graduated a year and a half before her and took a job in my hometown. We had a long distance relationship while she finished up her degree. I would make the five hour drive on the weekends to see her as much as I could. We got engaged and made a commitment to one another to stick it out during this time. Even with that I could feel like we were growing apart. Eventually Jaime graduated, and we got married soon after.

After tying the knot we decided to venture out on our own and moved away from family and ended up in Colorado Springs. Jaime took an unpaid internship to finish up requirements for her degree, and I hit the pavement looking for work. I spent the next month or so looking and burning up what little savings we had. I eventually got a job at a children's psychiatric hospital making $9.25 an hour. I took the bus to work every day. We struggled financially and were living in a place where we really had no support system.

After Jaime's internship ended she was able to get a job working retail. I worked during the week, and she would only get one weekend off a month. We were definitely the proverbial passing ships in the night. Our long distance relationship from the past two years was extending into our first year of marriage. It was an adventure but a lonely one at that. We had our fights and arguments as all newlyweds do trying to adjust to life together.

On our first anniversary I worked a double shift at the hospital and came home late only to find out that the bus lines didn't go all the way to our apartment. I had to walk the remaining few miles home at night and upon arriving found that our new puppy was not in her kennel and had trashed our apartment. I fell into the couch exhausted and knew something had to change.

We talked about how we didn't move out to Colorado to live like this. Things needed to change. The plan moving forward was to put our belongings in storage, get out of our lease, and to live out of our car hiking, rafting and climbing mountains. Things got better over the next couple of months as we spent time together. Eventually we had to come back to earth and start working again. We had put out job applications to places all over the west. During this time we were living in a friend's basement, and both of us took jobs at the psychiatric hospital where I had worked earlier.

Long story short we eventually got interviews at a boarding school in California and made the move to The Golden State. Things between us were better for a while, but we drifted apart again as work became our new priority. We stopped going to church, because our new jobs had us working most Sundays. I was growing apart from God and Jaime. I felt like I had become an afterthought in my own marriage. I struggled with sin and lust as well. I thought for some time in those first few years that we were headed for a divorce. It's not what I wanted, but nothing seemed to be working.

I realized eventually that the only true thing I had control over was how much I went after my relationship with God. I couldn't change my marriage on my own. I knew in my heart that He was the only truly trustworthy thing out there. I began to read my Bible and pray every day. I would pray for Jaime when we would go to sleep at night, and we still laugh about it to this day how she would without fail fall asleep on me in the middle of my prayers.

This seeking after God did not come without resistance. We still fought, and I struggled to remain consistent. I still wrestled with my flesh as well. When I look back I realize that it took two years of consistently seeking after God and putting Him first every day before I started to see things change in my marriage, and those changes did not come in the way I would have predicted. There was also a good deal of trial and persecution that went on during that time. The adversary did not want me to persevere and be blessed. What I can definitely say improved over that two year period was my communication with the Holy Spirit. It wasn't just me talking to God and asking for things, but our relationship moved to a place where I was listening. I was truly seeking Him and what He wanted from me.

Also during that period of time I went back to graduate school. Something I did during that decision process which I wouldn't recommend is that I only mentioned once to my wife that I was considering going back to school before applying and enrolling. This obviously caused some disagreement and arguing. She was not in support of the decision at the time, but I knew God was leading me to go back to school. I needed to learn to follow His lead even if it wasn't a popular or supported decision. I was beginning to understand that stepping out in faith and leading can be lonely and tough at times.

I gutted out the next few years working full time and going to school full time. This also included working internships for next to nothing, and basically having days in which I worked from 6:00am to 2:30pm and went to school until 10:00pm at night. God was good and kept me plugging away through it all. Upon graduating I was presented with the job opportunity to be fast-tracked into the school director position of the boarding school. I also had another job offer to do social work at a foster care agency. I prayed about it, and it was clear that I should take the social worker job. Jaime and I were not in agreement on this decision either. We argued about it, and I told her that God was pretty clear with me about which job to take.

After taking the foster care job the school that was offering me the director position closed down four months later, leaving my wife without a job. The God thing in all of it was that because I had spent the past few years making my time with Him a priority my spirit was becoming attuned to His voice and leading. I took the job that paid a lot less money despite the advice people were giving me, but four months later I still had a job. This was not a coincidence. Looking back on it things in my marriage began to change from that point forward as I began to trust my relationship with God and the decisions He was leading me to make, and consequently Jaime began to trust me in that process. Don't get me wrong we still have our battles and struggles, and we can both be pretty opinionated at times, but I don't feel like we are fighting one another in the process anymore. We have weathered a lot of storms over the past 20 plus years, but God has brought us closer through them, instead of them pushing us apart as they used to do.

2. Pastor

This aspect of one's team may seem controversial or unnecessary to some of you who are reading this. You might be saying to yourself "Why do I need a pastor? Can't I just pray and get my direction straight from God and the Bible?" Well I may know how to change my oil and do a brake job on my car, but I don't know how to do much else. I go to a mechanic for help with the rest of my car's needs. I know how to brush and floss my teeth, but I don't know how to do a root canal. Furthermore as a Christian, I know how to read my Bible and pray (somewhat at least), but I need someone to teach me and guide me in the deeper things of the faith. Another way to look it at would be the idea of a pastor being similar to the role of an assistant coach or an offensive or defensive coordinator or a specific positions coach. That person in the athletic arena helps explain and execute the plays of the playbook and specifically helps you with skills and techniques that you need to develop to become a better player in your position. Their job is to equip you for the field. Similarly in Ephesians 4:11-16 (New Living Translation) it says:

> Now these are the gifts Christ gave to the church: the apostles, the prophets, the evangelists, and the pastors and teachers. Their responsibility is to equip God's people to do his work and build up the church, the body of Christ. This will continue until we all come to such unity in our faith and knowledge of God's Son that we will be mature in the Lord, measuring up to the full and complete standard of Christ.

Then we will no longer be immature like children. We won't be tossed and blown about by every wind of new teaching. We will not be influenced when people try to trick us with lies so clever they sound like the truth. Instead, we will speak the truth in love, growing in every way more and more like Christ, who is the head of his body, the church. He makes the whole body fit together perfectly. As each part does its own special work, it helps the other parts grow, so that the whole body is healthy and growing and full of love.

As an athlete in order to be the best I could be I needed the advice, guidance, pushing and expertise that those coaches and specialists brought to my game. I need the same thing in my life today from pastors and teachers who know me, instruct me and challenge me, so that I can be equipped and mature.

I have grown up in the church and have continued to attend and be under the teaching of a pastor throughout my life. I've had good church experiences and bad ones. I have sat under good teaching and some not-so-good teaching. I have also had times where the Holy Spirit has directed me to leave a church because of some sinful practices that were occurring, but I have never given up on going to church. In Psalm 92:13-14 (New King James Version) it says "Those who are planted in the house of the Lord shall flourish in the courts of our God. They shall still bear fruit in old age; they shall be fresh and flourishing." God wants me to be planted in His house being taught by one of His shepherds, so that I can flourish and bear fruit.

On my journey in life thus far when it comes to church and pastors I have seen a continuum with many people's views where there is pastor worship (idolizing the person more than God) on one end, and there is an overtly critical or even vilifying spirit on the other end. It is important to understand that pastors are humans and put their pants on the same way you and I do every morning. They may be called by God to devote their life to the studying and teaching of God's word, but they still have the same battle with the sin nature in order to live it out. We have to be careful to not make these people our King Saul (1 Samuel 8:4-21). So how does one know how to find a good pastor? God gives us some criteria in the following:

This is a trustworthy saying: "If someone aspires to a church leader, he desires an honorable position." So a church leader must be a man whose life is above reproach. He must be faithful to his wife. He must exercise self-control, live wisely, and have a good reputation. He must enjoy having guests in his home, and he must be able to teach. He must not be a heavy drinker or be violent. He must be gentle, not quarrelsome and not love money. He must manage his own family well, having children who respect and obey him. For if a man cannot manage his own household, how can he take care of God's church?

A church leader must not be a new believer, because he might become proud, and the devil would cause him to fall. Also, people outside the church must speak well of him so that he will not be disgraced and fall into the devil's trap. (1 Timothy 3:1-6 New Living Translation)

All of these attributes are ways to measure or determine if this person is trustworthy and someone you should be "planted" under. We need to be vigilant and discerning in this regard and not jump to the next flashy personality. Jesus warns us of this as well when he says:

"Beware of false prophets who come to you in sheep's clothing but inwardly are ravaging wolves. You'll recognize them by their fruit. Are grapes gathered from thornbushes or figs from thistles? In the same way, every good tree produces good fruit, but a bad tree produces bad fruit. A good tree can't produce bad fruit; neither can a bad tree produce good fruit. Every tree that doesn't produce good fruit is cut down and thrown into the fire. So you'll recognize them by their fruit." (Matthew 7:15-19 Holman Christian Standard Bible)

Jesus knows that the devil is going to plant bad fruit in His church. There are going to be "ravaging wolves" in the sheepfold. Jesus had this issue on His own team with Judas, and he addresses this and His plan for it in the Parable of the Wheat and the Tares (Matthew 13:24-30). We need to prayerfully discern and analyze the fruit and life of our pastoral leaders and determine if it is in line with the word of God. It is our decision to determine where we are planted (with God's help and leading). I don't have a magic formula for this decision, and I am not saying that we hold anyone to a level of perfection. Jesus didn't say that either. He didn't say perfect fruit. He said they produce "good fruit." We are able to recognize this by the fruit of that person's life. Sometimes I need to remember a banana or an apple with a few bruises on it is still good for you.

3. Veteran Players

Have you ever wondered why a coach or general manager or owner will put a team together that consists of younger players and older or veteran players? If you look at it from a purely athletic, speed and strength viewpoint it doesn't make sense to have older players on a team. They're slower and more prone to injury. A lot of older players on professional teams do a great job of keeping themselves in shape and able to compete, but the reality is athletically they aren't ever going to be what they used to be. It's an inevitable truth. So why do teams keep older players or sometimes trade for them towards the end of their careers? What does a veteran player provide for a team that can help bring them success? It is their leadership which comes from wisdom and experience that only those players can provide which is invaluable to the team culture. Those players keep the younger players calm and focused. They have played through the ups and downs, the winning seasons and the losing seasons. They have worked through injuries and competed in high stress games and situations. Their mindset is what is wanted and valued in those locker rooms.

If it is important for the culture of any sports team to have those veteran players, then we should be keeping that in mind when it comes to who we have on our teams today. However societally it seems to be consistently moving further away from the value that older "players" in our lives should be important to us. Newer is better. There is a technology update on our phones every week it seems. There is a new version of our phones or laptops we need to upgrade every year in order to remain relevant. We seem to listen more and more to the opinions of the young and the beautiful. Our TVs and computers are blasted with their videos all the time in a steady non-stop stream. Status and esteem seem to be based off of how many subscribers or views one gets, not in the character or accomplishments of one's life. We have immediate answers to questions right at our fingertips. Sometimes it seems we live in a world full of knowledge that is bereft of wisdom.

In Job 12:12 (New Living Translation) it says "Wisdom belongs to the aged, and understanding to the old." Also in Proverbs 20:29 (New Living Translation) it says "The glory of the young is their strength; the gray hair of experience is the splendor of the old." So it would seem if we are to value wisdom and experience and want that on our team in this life, it comes from "the old." It comes from those veteran players who have seen it and done it. King Solomon understood this. According to scripture God granted Solomon more wisdom than any other man (1 Kings 3:7-12). So if you were the world's wisest man you would probably be pretty good in the wisdom department right? Well it says in

1 Kings 12:6 (Good News Translation), talking about Solomon's son, that "King Rehoboam consulted the older men who had served as his father Solomon's advisers." So yes in case you didn't think you read that right, the world's wisest man had advisers. Who were his advisers? Older men.

We still need to be careful in our choices, however just because someone is older than you does not mean they are wise. Again we need to prayerfully consider what veteran players God wants us to put on our team, and this is also done by examining the kind of fruit they produce. If I want someone on my team who can help me grow financially, then I shouldn't choose someone who is broke. How about someone to help you in your marriage or with parenting? You probably don't want someone who has had multiple divorces, cheats on their wife and their kids hate them. Again we are not looking for perfect fruit. We are looking for good fruit.

So where do you find and recruit these veteran players for your team? Well these older players are around if we're looking for them. They could be someone at our work, someone in our families, someone at our church, someone at our gym, someone in our neighborhood, etc. I have been blessed to have some Godly and wise men in my family that I speak with and also some guys at my church's men's group. Some of these men I see weekly, and some I speak to on a monthly basis or less. I'm able to vent to them a bit and ask them for advice on things. A question I have posed to many of them is this "Looking back what advice would you give someone my age?" I am asking this so I can avoid some pitfalls in my life and gather wisdom from their experience. I want to know from some of these veteran players how to have longevity in the game.

So in closing let's remember that we will become the people we are around. As I stated earlier in the chapter none us had a choice of the family we grew up in, but we do have a choice now when it comes to the people we put in our lives. Choose your team wisely.

Chapter 7

<u>Who Is Not On Your Team?</u>

"Boundaries define us. They define what is me and what is not me. A boundary shows me where I end and someone else begins, leading me to a sense of ownership. Knowing what I am to own and take responsibility for gives me freedom."

-Henry Cloud

      I am going to take a slightly different thought process in this chapter when it comes to the idea of who is not on your team. The *who* is not going to be a person or persons. The *who* we are going to look at is the team that we allow to reside in our mind and spirit that is detrimental and sometimes outright destructive to our lives. My angle on this comes from the following two sections of scripture and some of my work with people over the years as a psychotherapist.

1. Therefore, since we are surrounded by such a huge crowd of witnesses to the life of faith, let us strip off every weight that slows us down, especially the sin that so easily trips us up. And let us run with endurance the race God has set before us (Hebrews 12:1 New Living Translation).

      The picture being painted here is that of a runner in a race in front of a cheering crowd. I can relate to this imagery as a track athlete who ran competitively for many years. I can also relate as an athlete in terms of honing my body to get rid of any excess weight that would slow me down and not allow me to compete at my best. This verse is speaking to that concept spiritually. What mindset or sin am I allowing in my life that trips me up? That gets in the way of me competing at my best?

      This concept became very clear to me in a new way when I attempted to thru-hike the John Muir Trail in the summer of 2018. For those of you who don't know what the John Muir Trail is (or the "JMT" as it's called), it's a 211 mile long trail with 47,000 feet of elevation change that stretches from the Yosemite Valley to Mount Whitney in the Sierra Nevada mountain range in California. As my competitive athletic career winded down in my early 20s, and I graduated college I spent more time pursuing outdoor athletics such as backpacking, rock climbing and skiing. I had always loved doing those things but often didn't have the time due to my other obligations and also didn't want to explain to my coaches if I happened to get injured doing those activities. Also in terms of skiing I was forbidden by my parents to do that sport as a child, because they were afraid I'd like it and it was too expensive for them to afford. In any case being in nature and God's creation has always been a very important boost to my psyche and soul, and I try to get a dose of it every day.

For the first four years that we lived in California Jaime had a job leading backpack trips for high school aged kids at a boarding school. I would see all these amazing pictures of places throughout the state as she would be out there for close to two weeks at a time. I realized that even though I had seen and experienced a lot of what the state had to offer there was so much of it that could only be accessed by hiking to it. I thought about it, and it seemed like doing the JMT would be the best way to experience all of that. Now mind you of all of the outdoor activities I do backpacking is the least fun in my book. It's a lot of work and struggle and something I wonder why I'm doing it while I'm in the middle of it, but a lot of things in life are like that.

I have a friend who was quite experienced in the backpacking world who I approached with the idea. Backpacking was his thing, and the Sierras were his spot, so it didn't take much convincing when I proposed the idea. He was on board. To be truthful I had done my fair share of backpacking in the past, but this was my first introduction into the world of what is known as ultralight backpacking. He explained to me that the goal was to get your whole set up (food, water, clothes, tent, sleeping bag/pad, stove, backpack, etc) under 25 pounds. He had a scale that weighed ounces, and we scrutinized every piece of gear to try and pair it down.

We ended up getting a permit for the hike heading south to north starting in Cottonwood Pass which took us approximately two days of hiking to get to the starting point of the trail at the summit of Mount Whitney. To get this thing done with kids and careers and such, our plan was to do the whole hike in 15 days. If you do the math, that means a lot of miles each day with no rest days. We would pack four to five days of food at a time and stop for a resupply. The concept of "stripping off every weight" became clearer to me every time we hit one of those food resupplies.

For me while I was doing this hike there was never a time that some part of my body didn't hurt. The discomfort just moved from spot to spot: shoulders to back to knees to calves to feet and back again. I thought that there would be a time when my body would adjust, and I wouldn't feel that pain, but it never happened. The one thing I did realize is that the less and less weight I carried, the less discomfort I felt. I started to take inventory of what food I was eating and what I wasn't. I started to really look at what gear I was using and what I wasn't, and by the time I got to the second resupply I downsized my things to only the absolute essentials. I "stripped off every weight that slowed me down." I thought in the beginning of this whole endeavor that the ounce counting seemed a bit ridiculous, but when I got halfway through I was convinced it was necessary.

With the support of friends and family and a lot of pushing through the pain we did accomplish our goal of hiking the JMT in 15 days. As I said it gave me a fresh perspective on Hebrews 12:1, and I've asked myself what are the weights and sins I'm carrying now that weigh me down and trip me up? Why do I continue to hold on to them through the ups and downs of life? Why don't I strip them away, so I can "run with endurance the race God has set before" me?

2. For though we walk in the flesh, we do not war according to the flesh. For the weapons of our warfare are not carnal but mighty in God for pulling down strongholds, casting down arguments and every high thing that exalts itself against the knowledge of God, bringing every thought into captivity to the obedience of Christ (2 Corinthians 10:3-5 New King James Version).

These "strongholds" and "thoughts" and "things that exalt itself against the knowledge of God" are some of the "weights" from Hebrews 12:1 that I see all the time in the lives of so many people I talk to and in my own life. We often only focus on certain sins and hindrances in our lives and fail to really look at the mindsets that hold us back. It is these mindsets or strongholds that are tricky and often multi-generational, and the devil uses these to steal our lives. It is these thoughts about ourselves and others that are not from God and His word that we let on our *team* each day which weigh us down. This list isn't exhaustive by any means and won't apply to everyone, but let's take a look at some of these and pray for God's supernatural grace as we seek to pull down these strongholds in our lives.

An Unforgiving and Judgmental Heart

This one is a biggie. It is so hard to root out, because we as a society feel entitled to our pain. We feel entitled to our complaints. We often feel we got the wrong end of the stick. We want to carry it with us like a security blanket without recognizing how it completely weighs us down. It feels right to be angry at someone who has hurt us. It's a natural response after all and a protective measure for us, so that we don't get hurt again. That makes sense right?

As a therapist I speak with patients all the time who have been hurt and wounded and carry those wounds with them, sometimes for the entirety of their lives. Others lose decades of their lives holding on to hurt. They are completely resistant to the topic of forgiveness. They say things like "Are you kidding me? That person doesn't deserve my forgiveness." I tell them I agree, but that forgiveness is for them, not their offender. It sometimes works but oftentimes it doesn't. The Bible has a lot to say about forgiveness which we'll get to in a bit, but I wanted to take a moment and look at what Jesus has to say about judging others and how that relates to an unforgiving heart in the area of interpersonal conflict.

In Matthew 7:1-5 (New International Version) it says "Do not judge, or you too will be judged. For in the same way you judge others, you will be judged, and with the measure you use, it will be measured to you. Why do you look at the speck of sawdust in your brother's eye and pay no attention to the plank in your own eye? How can you say to your brother, 'Let me take the speck out of your eye,' when all the time there is a plank in your own eye? You hypocrite, first take the plank out of your own eye, and then you will see clearly to remove the speck from your brother's eye."

This is an amazing lesson taught by Jesus that we all should really let sink in, but here is my thought using these two word pictures of the plank and the speck Jesus gives us when it comes to forgiveness. I often see people when there is an argument or conflict, and the two sides have wronged one another. The one side who is offended and feels justified in their actions towards the other person often thinks they don't need to apologize or forgive. Why is that? Could it be because they are comparing offenses and they see a log in someone else's eye and think they only have a speck in their own eye? They think to themselves "I know I did or said something I shouldn't have, but what they did to me was so much worse. Until they say they're sorry I'm not going to clean up my side in this." The problem is one of comparison and an unwillingness to deal with the "speck."

I used to work construction and when you are building and get a speck of sawdust in your eye, the first thing you do is try to get it out. If you don't get it out it becomes irritated and infected, and you could cause permanent damage to that eye. A permanently damaged eye affects your whole system. This is the issue with our unwillingness to clean up our side and to apologize even if we think the other person's offense is so much greater than our own. The speck just doesn't go away. It actually has the potential to ruin our whole system and often does.

I understand this is an example of when two parties are in the wrong, and there are definite times when someone is hurt or abused through no fault of their own. However Jesus still calls us to forgive in these situations. In fact a lot of us reading this book can probably recite the Lord's Prayer or have heard it a few times.

> Our Father which art in heaven hallowed be thy name. Thy kingdom come, thy will be done, on earth as it is in Heaven (Matthew 6:8-9 King James Version)."

Recognize those words? I'm sure many of you do. If you jump forward a verse or two in Matthew 6:12 (New International Version) it says "And forgive us our debts, as we also have forgiven our debtors." Notice the word "forgiven." I am not an English teacher, so I apologize if I botch this, however the word forgiven is a past participle. A past participle indicates a past or completed action or time. In that light then what this verse is saying is that if we want God to "forgive us our debts," then we need to have already forgiven our debtors. That is a hard truth for me to swallow, but the point of it is that we are supposed to be ever mindful of the debt God paid for us, and in that light we will freely forgive others. In short, if we want God to forgive us, then we need to forgive others.

There are many other places where the Bible addresses the topic of forgiveness. Here's a couple more:

Bear with each other and forgive one another if any of you has a grievance against someone. Forgive as the Lord forgave you (Colossians 3:13 New International Version).

Do not judge others, and you will not be judged. Do not condemn others, or it will all come back against you. Forgive others, and you will be forgiven (Luke 6:37 New Living Translation).

So how do you keep an unforgiving and judgmental heart off of your team?

I am no expert on this. There are many great books out there on this subject. One that I have found extremely helpful and challenging on this subject is *The Bait of Satan* by John Bevere. Check it out if this stronghold is especially hard for you.

The following are my two cents on what has worked for me, but I want to start off by saying that rooting out an unforgiving heart is really hard work and needs to be done on an almost daily basis. There are so many opportunities in our daily lives to be hurt and offended by others. The devil knows this and uses it on us all the time. I often need to remind myself that we are all in process. We are works in progress. None of us are perfect. I try to remember that old saying "Please be patient. God isn't finished with me yet."

1. **Recognize that you've been hurt**- This may seem obvious, but it isn't. Very often we (especially as men) won't admit to ourselves that we've been hurt by someone. We just shrug it off, or so we think. We actually stuff it down, and the hurt surfaces when we don't want it to and in ways we often can't control. So do yourself a favor and just admit to yourself that someone hurt you.
2. **Pray**- We need to recognize that the way God wants us to forgive is impossible to do without Him. Without His grace involved in it, we won't be able to do it. So pray and ask for help.
3. **Process**- I often do this when I am hiking very early in the morning in the woods when no one else is around, and I can audibly talk to God through how I'm feeling. In Luke 5:16 (New Living Translation) it says "But Jesus often withdrew to the wilderness for prayer." In my processing with God I tell Him what happened. In essence I vent. I want to get to the thoughts and feelings out of my head and in front of me so to speak, so that I can analyze them. Are my feelings justified? Am I overreacting? What is the other person's point of view on this?
4. **Forgive and Cast It Off**- After processing things I pray to forgive that person, and I cast the weight of their offense off of me. In 1 Peter 5:7 (New King James Version) it says "casting all your care upon Him, for He cares for you." I know it may seem a little odd, but often times I make a throwing motion with my arm as if I am casting that burden off of myself and at Jesus' feet.

5. **Bless**- The issue when someone has hurt you or used you is that something has been taken from you, and it's out of your control to get it back. As much as we'd like sometimes we cannot control what other people do to us. A way to take control back (which is counterintuitive but is Biblical) is to pray a blessing for the person who has offended you (Romans 12:14-21 New International Version). God instructs in verse 19 where He says "It is mine to avenge. I will repay." God is pretty good in the justice department. Trust it. Simply ask Him to bless that person in order to take back control in that area of your life, and let God do what He does.

6. **Clean Up**- I don't like this one, but it often take two to tango as the saying goes. In Psalm 139:24 (Holman Christian Standard Bible) it says "See if there is any offensive way in me; lead me in the everlasting way." Notice the word "any." It doesn't specify if it's a "speck" or a "log." Often times we get hurt in arguments or when our expectations aren't met, and we do or say something we shouldn't to the other person. God calls us to apologize and clean that up, regardless of the other person's offense towards you. I have often been led by the Spirit after a fight with my wife to draw near to her and repent when that is the absolute last thing I want to do.

7. **Confront** (if possible or appropriate)- I caution you on this one. Sometimes it is appropriate to confront the person who offended you and forgive, but often times it isn't. It depends on the level of the relationship. If it's your spouse or one of people on your team that sees the "good, bad and ugly" of you, then it's appropriate and will deepen your relationship. If not we need to be careful of our motives on this one. Often times people will say to someone "I forgive you for hurting me when you _____." This isn't done to forgive the person. It's done as a way of you making sure that person knows they did something wrong to you. It's how you get your jab in on them. You haven't forgiven and casted it off. You're still hurt and angry. Check yourself there. In 1 Corinthians 13:4-5 (New International Version) it says "Love is patient, love is kind. It does not envy, it does not boast, it is not proud. It does not dishonor others, it is not self-seeking, it is not easily angered, it keeps no record of wrongs." This is a God kind of love. This is something we need His help to walk out in our lives.

8. **Boundaries**- Sometimes at the end of this forgiveness process we need to establish some different boundaries. God calls us to forgive others, but He doesn't say we need to be best friends or be friends at all. If someone is continuing to

hurt you and not respect you, then move on. Sometimes we hold on to toxic people and situations much longer than we should, and we need to shed that weight to better run our race. Sometimes we need to redefine our own expectations or boundaries with ourselves when it comes to what we expect from that other person. An amazing book on this subject is actually called *Boundaries* by Henry Cloud and John Townsend.

Now let's talk for a minute about a judgmental heart. I know we looked at how judging others connects to an unforgiving heart, but in my line of work I witness a lot of people who are stuck with the weight of constantly judging themselves. It's a very debilitating cycle which some or most of you might relate to. "I don't like this or that about myself." "I wish I would have done this or that differently." "Looking back if I only would have done things this way." There seems to be a back and forth between perfectionism and regret which can be quite a prison of the mind that has the potential to steal your joy and paralyze your life. The devil wants us stuck in this place.

I relate it to a situation where an opposing player talks trash or taunts you and gets you to doubt yourself and your skills. That player gets you off your game. What happens next is you start making poor decisions; you make bad passes or you start missing shots. The poor play reinforces your negative thoughts about yourself, and you continue to perform less than your capabilities. I'm pretty sure we've all been there a time or two in our athletic careers. Sometimes it takes a few minutes in a game situation to shrug it off and sometimes it takes days, weeks or months to get it back. Some players can never shake it, and it can ruin their confidence and athletic career for good.

If you do an internet search about self-judgment, the antidote to self-judgment in the world of psychotherapy seems to be self-acceptance. I don't completely disagree with this on its face. I agree there are a lot of things we need to learn to accept about ourselves and the way God has made us, but I think it falls short. The idea of self-acceptance is still based on the "self" as the word says. I don't know about you, but my "self" can be pretty fickle. It seems to change day to day, hour to hour and sometimes minute to minute. Some days I like myself, and some days I can't stand myself. And if I go back to my sports metaphor that I mentioned in the last paragraph, then the antidote of doing this on your own through the process of self-acceptance doesn't quite cut it.

Picture for yourself that you're in the middle of a game, and the opposing defender has been able to stop you each time you face one another. He's been talking trash, and your confidence is ebbing away. You give yourself a little positive self-talk in your head ("C'mon! You got this!"), however it doesn't seem to be helping. What typically happens next? Yep, the coach calls a time out. The coach calls you to the sideline in order to regroup. He may pull you to the side and ask if everything is alright. Then the coach will say something to this effect, "Okay shake it off. You got this. Do what you've practiced. Play your game. Block out the noise and get to work." He gives a quick pep talk in order to refocus you, and then sends you back out on the field.

God does the same thing with His players. When the voices of self-judgment rise up in our heads and the devil is beating you up, we need to call a time-out and regroup. You don't just continue playing the game allowing your opponent to win every match up, however that is what we do when we live in a state of constant self-judgment. We also know what happens next as players if we don't listen to the coach after the time-out and get our game back in order. We get taken out of the game. We get benched, and another player takes our place on the field. And that is precisely what the devil wants for your life.

So how do we fight against this?

Remember as you read earlier in the chapter in 2 Corinthians 10:5 (New King James Version) it states that we bring "every thought into captivity to the obedience of Christ." Those thoughts include our negative self-judgments. I like to run those thoughts through the filter of John 10:10 (English Standard Version) where it says "The thief (devil) comes only to steal and kill and destroy; I (Jesus) came that they may have life and have it abundantly." So from this verse I ask myself "Is what I am feeling or thinking about myself stealing, killing or destroying my life? Or is it giving me abundant life?" So let's address those thoughts that are destroying our lives.

In Matthew 18:18 (New International Version) it says "Truly I tell you, whatever you bind on earth will be bound in heaven, and whatever you loose on earth will be loosed in heaven." So what does this mean and how does it apply? Let's look at the same verse in in the New Living Translation. "I tell you the truth, whatever you forbid on earth will be forbidden in heaven, and whatever you permit on earth will be permitted in heaven." So bind can mean forbid and loose can mean permit. In this chapter Jesus is giving this heavenly authority to His disciples and to you and me as well as His followers. I can "bind" (forbid, stop) the thoughts that steal, kill or destroy my life in the name of Jesus, and I can "loose" (permit, allow) His thoughts and vision over my life.

Here are a few examples from God's playbook:

I bind the lie that I am gripped by fear and loose a spirit of power, love and a sound mind (2 Timothy 1:7).

I bind the lie that I lack confidence and loose the truth of "being confident of this, that he who began a good work in you will carry it on to completion until the day of Christ Jesus (Philippians 1:6 New International Version)."

I bind anxiety and loose the peace of God (Philippians 4:6-7).

I bind lack and loose God's provision (Philippians 4:19).

So what am I permitting and what am I forbidding to take space in my thoughts and in my mind?

I only have so much mental real estate, so I need to bind those thoughts and judgments that are not of God and practice what the Coach says about me and my life. Permit and practice those thoughts, and in doing so we begin to transform and renew our minds (Romans 12:2). Also keep in mind in Romans 8:1 (English Standard Version) where it says "There is therefore now no condemnation to those who are in Christ Jesus." If the negative thoughts and self-judgments in your mind are condemning you, they are not of God. We need to deal with them.

These self-judgments are strongholds. If I were to mention a couple of other strongholds, you would be pretty clear as to what someone is to do about those things. So let's say for instance the strongholds of adultery or drug abuse. If you were giving advice to someone dealing with those issues, you might tell them that they need to stop (forbid, bind) that extramarital affair or stop (forbid, bind) abusing heroin for example. They need to repent and get back to God's game plan in those areas of their life. It seems pretty clear right? Those things are clear sinful actions that harm that person and others in that person's life. How come we don't apply the same thought process to the negative self-judgments in our lives? We tolerate them and often feed them multiple times throughout our daily lives. We don't see them as sin that needs repentance.

In Ezekiel 18:30-31 (English Standard Version) it says "Repent and turn from *all* your transgressions, lest iniquity be your ruin. Cast away from you *all* the transgressions that you have committed, and make yourselves a new heart and a new spirit!" A transgression is defined as an act that goes against a law, rule or code of conduct; an offense. The verse says "turn from *all* your transgressions." "Cast away from you *all* the transgressions." That means all of them. For example, if I believe that I am created in the image of God (Genesis 1:27) and that I am fearfully and wonderfully made by Him (Psalm 139:14) but spend all kinds of time in my mind and with my mouth putting myself down, how is that not an offense or a transgression against God who made me? We need to "repent, turn and cast away" first, and then we can make ourselves "a new heart and a new spirit." Tell God you're sorry for all the ways you've judged yourself. Ask for forgiveness. Bind it each time it comes up and create that new spirit.

The next verse in this passage is Ezekiel 18:32 where it says "For I have no pleasure in the death of anyone, declares the Lord God; so turn, and live." Turn and live. Turn from this weight of an unforgiving and judgmental heart.

Making Excuses/Lack of Discipline

This next weight we allow on our team connects in some ways to the one we just discussed in the area of a judgmental heart. Many of the judgments we hold on ourselves come from a place of making excuses for ourselves and a lack of discipline in our lives. Some of you might be thinking that statement is a bit harsh, but let's look at it and see if the shoe fits. Obviously there are a number of things in our lives we can't do much about, but there are quite a few things that are in our control. As we just talked about in the last section when we say or think some negative judgmental thing about ourselves we need to repent and ask for forgiveness, however there is an issue if we just stop there. I can have the faith that God can heal me and help me, but if I don't do anything myself, then it won't matter. It's pretty clear in James 2:17 (New King James Version) where it says "faith by itself, if it does not have works, is dead." I can believe in something, but I also need to do something about it.

1. Physical Discipline

So let's talk for a minute about our physical health. We all can agree that when we are physically healthy and feeling strong, our mental state follows suit. We tend to be less judgmental of ourselves, and maybe we actually like the person we see in the mirror every day. The issue in my line of work and in the mindset of a lot of people is that we are too focused on our feelings. Our emotions or feelings too often dictate our behaviors. We don't feel like it, so we don't do it. We get stuck in our heads and don't do the things we know we should. Some of us as Christians may be familiar with the concept in 1 Corinthians 6:19 of our bodies being the temple of the Holy Spirit. The context is in reference to sexual purity, but I think it goes further than that.

> "Or didn't you realize that your body is a sacred place, the place of the Holy Spirit? Don't you see that you can't live however you please, squandering what God paid such a high price for? The physical part of you is not some piece of property belonging to the spiritual part of you. God owns the whole works. So let people see God in and through your body (1 Corinthians 6:19 The Message)."

Or let's look at Romans 6:12-13 (New Living Translation):

> "Do not let sin control the way you live; do not give in to sinful desires. Do not let any part of your body become an instrument of evil to serve sin. Instead, give yourselves completely to God, for you were dead, but now you have new life. So use your whole body as an instrument to do what is right for the glory of God."

This next weight we need to strip off is making excuses and a lack of discipline in our lives. When we were athletes, discipline was definitely our friend. We might not have liked it, but we depended on it. We all let ourselves go a little in the offseason, but when it came time to compete we had to be on. Our minds and bodies needed to be operating at full capacity. We were conscious of what we ate, how much time we slept and our workout routines. If we weren't aware and doing those things we wouldn't survive out on the field. An issue I had in my own life after my athletic career ended was that I invited a lack of discipline onto my team. I will get into some of the details of that later in the book, but I have seen how important that is for my mind, body and spirit as I've grown older. I have also seen how important it is for my marriage, my kids, my work and my leadership. When I am disciplined physically I am operating in the way God designed my body to be and am able to accomplish what He has for me to do. When I am physically healthy I can be fully present for God and the people He has put in my life.

Paul spoke of this as well in 1 Corinthians 9:27 (New Living Translation) when he wrote "I discipline my body like an athlete, training it to do what it should. Otherwise, I fear that after preaching to others I myself might be disqualified." Paul is referring to self-discipline in this section of scripture in terms of keeping a check on our sin nature, but the same principle applies to our health and physical discipline.

It seems like no accident that the original sin and temptation in the Garden of Eden was about food. I'm going to get on my soapbox for a bit for this next section. I apologize if this offends you, but I think it needs to be said. I have grown up in the church and still go every week. Throughout my whole life (and yes there have been some exceptions to this but not many) pastors and churches have always warned us against these big sins: drinking alcohol, smoking, drugs, sex before or outside marriage, profanity and pornography. I know there are a few more on the list, but you get my gist. I fully agree that these things will be very destructive to your life and have been in my own at times. The formula always seems to be though, if I avoid these things then I will have a happy and healthy life regardless of whatever else I do to my health or body. I can eat or drink whatever I want and as much as I want, as long as it's not alcohol. Often times in the American church it seems okay for someone to drink two liters of soda a day but not okay to have a glass of wine at dinner. It's not very often we hear from the pulpit warning against things like: overeating, obesity, binge watching TV, binging on social media, lethargy, sloth or taking excessive medications that are avoidable through diet and lifestyle changes.

This is a major issue in our society as a whole, but how is the church addressing it? How are we as the body of Christ setting the example?

According to the Center for Disease Control's (CDC) website page on Chronic Disease in America, six in 10 adults have one chronic disease and four in 10 have two. Chronic diseases include conditions like heart disease, cancer, lung disease, stroke, diabetes, kidney disease, and Alzheimer's. The page also lists four key lifestyle risks that greatly contribute to these diseases: tobacco use, poor nutrition, lack of physical activity and excessive alcohol use ("Chronic Disease in America," 2019). I'm not sure if you caught that but 60 percent of adults in America have at least one chronic disease. Most of these can be prevented by a healthy diet and lifestyle throughout our lives. The devil is deceiving us on this one. I'm not a doctor or a physical trainer or a nutritionist, but easily the majority of us have access to one in order to start putting some of these disciplines into practice. This is definitely a "weight" that is slowing a lot of us down.

If you want to tell me after reading this that you don't have time to work out or make your lunch or buy actual real unprocessed food, then check yourself. Drop the weight of excuses off your team. Did you know there are settings on your phone that will tell you how much time you spend daily on your phone? Go ahead and check it out. I think you'll be shocked at how much time you spend staring at a screen in your hand. I also talk to a lot of my patients about being aware of how much time they *think* about working out or *think about* complaining about themselves, and my reframe for them is to actually *do* something healthy during that time instead. You could go for a ten minute walk instead of thinking about how much you don't like your body. You could stretch or do jumping jacks or push-ups while you watch TV. You could park at the back of the parking lot when you go shopping and make sure you get more steps in. Get a standing desk at work. Go outside with your kids and play with them when they ask you to. Don't overcomplicate things. Don't let the devil steal your health. Honor God with your temple.

2. Financial Discipline

This next topic of discipline won't be a popular one either, but it can be such a heavy weight for so many of us in our lives. I know it has been in my life at times, and that's financial discipline. I am not a financial adviser and have learned a lot of these lessons the hard way. There are a ton of really smart financial people and books out there, and the Bible also has a lot to say about this subject as well. Actually the Bible talks about the subject of finances over 2300 times. God is trying to get our attention on this one. Jesus says in Matthew 6:24 (New International Version) that "No one can serve two masters. Either you will hate the one and love the other, or you will be devoted to the one and despise the other. You cannot serve both God and money."

A synonym for the word serve is obey. The first time the word worship is introduced in the Bible is in the context of obedience in Genesis 22 when Abraham is tested by God and asked to sacrifice his son Isaac. In Genesis 22:5 (New King James Version) Abraham tells his servants "Stay here with the donkey; the lad and I will go yonder and worship, and we will come back to you." Abraham is worshipping God through his obedience to Him. God never intended for Abraham to sacrifice Isaac, but He was testing his obedience. And that is the heart of worship, our obedience. If you jump ahead to verse 14 it is the also the first time in scripture that God's name as Provider (Jehovah Jireh) is introduced, after God provides Abraham with a ram to offer as his sacrifice. This is no coincidence and is key to our relationship with money and financial discipline.

God is our provider, and we worship Him through our obedience. If we don't see that, then we will serve or obey or worship money and not Him.

The word worship associated with money may seem a little strong, but I think it sits at the heart of this issue. It speaks to where we think our provision comes from. Does it come from God or me? Does God provide or do I? If I answer God, then I will do what He says when it comes to money. I will obey Him. If not, I'll do what I want. It's my money after all, right? So let's substitute the word worship for serve in Matthew 6:24 (New International Version) and see how it fits. "No one can *worship* two masters. Either you will hate the one and love the other, or you will be devoted to the one and despise the other. You cannot *worship* both God and money." So I need to start there and ask myself, "What do I worship?"

Money is a tricky one, because you need it to survive. It would be similar to a food addiction in that sense, since you also need food to survive. It's different than drugs or alcohol or gambling, since we don't need those. Food is not cocaine, but it can still trigger an increase in dopamine transmission in the brain's reward pathway, which is why when you eat a big greasy burger you often crave another one even though you're full. The accumulation and spending of wealth can do the same thing in the reward system in our brains.

So why does Jesus specifically call out money in the verse above and not any of these other things? Why doesn't He say you cannot serve both God and food or drugs or alcohol? Why money?

Our money and the accumulation of it can be directly connected to what we talked about in Chapter 3 when Jesus was tempted by the devil in the wilderness. If we serve money, it becomes connected to our flesh, ego and pride. It feeds our flesh because "I can buy and do what I want when I want" with money. It flaunts our ego because our "stuff (material goods, cars, houses, etc.)" often equates to our status in the world's eyes ("Look at what I can do"). Finally our wealth feeds our pride like no other. The more money and power I get, "the less I think I need God." This has been the case throughout history. The pride and ego aspects of money is also what set it apart from the other addictions listed above. With the other addictions there is often the feeling of shame involved. Someone who is addicted to drugs, alcohol, food, or even sex engages in their addictive behavior to avoid feelings of shame. Also if they are caught in these behaviors, they experience feelings of shame. This doesn't seem to be the case with wealth. In fact in our society and in societies throughout history, the accumulation and spending of wealth has always been praised. We look up to the rich and powerful. We often envy them. So there isn't that feeling of shame involved. It's actually a feeling of pride. The deeper I go into serving money, the more prideful I become. Our accumulation of wealth is reinforced by society. The richer I become, the more I am praised. That dynamic is not at play for someone who is addicted to these other things. The people stuck in those addictions are typically looked down upon, not esteemed.

I am not saying that money and the accumulation of wealth is a bad thing, just like I am not saying that food is a bad thing. It is the state of our heart towards those things. What do we worship? In 1 Timothy 6:9-10 (New Living Translation) it says "But people who long to be rich fall into temptation and are trapped by many foolish and harmful desires that plunge them into ruin and destruction. For the love of money is the root of all kinds of evil. And some people, craving money, have wandered from the true faith and pierced themselves with many sorrows." 1 Timothy is a letter from Paul written to his protégé Timothy. Timothy is pastoring the church in Ephesus at the time the letter is written, so the verses above are written as a warning to believers. From these verses it is vitally important that we analyze our relationship with money through God's game plan in order to *not*:

1. Fall into temptation
2. Be trapped by many foolish and harmful desires
3. Be plunged into ruin and destruction
4. Wander from the true faith
5. Pierce ourselves with many sorrows

This is a pretty alarming list. It's almost like God is yelling at us to not jump off a cliff or run out in traffic.

If we jump a few verses ahead in 1 Timothy 6:17-19 Paul provides a contrast in perspective in his instructions to Timothy in regards to wealth when he writes "Teach those who are rich in this world not to be proud and not to trust in their money, which is so unreliable. Their trust should be in God, who richly gives us all we need for our enjoyment. Tell them to use their money to do good. They should be rich in good works and generous to those in need, always being ready to share with others. By doing this they will be storing up their treasures as a good foundation for the future so that they may experience true life." So the contrasting view encourages us to:

1. Not be proud and trust in our money
2. Trust in God
3. Use our money to do good

4. Be rich in good works
5. Be generous
6. Be ready to share with others

Our mindset towards money will determine what we worship and directly correlates to our financial discipline. If we are serving money it will be impossible for us to be financially disciplined the way God has designed. It has to start there. In Ecclesiastes 5:10 (New International Version) it says "Whoever loves money never has enough; whoever loves wealth is never satisfied with their income. This too is meaningless." So if I am always chasing more money in order to feel satisfied, then I know who I am serving.

The wisdom literature from the book of Proverbs also provides some great insight into the area of financial discipline.

Get a Job

Those who work their land will have abundant food, but those who chase fantasies have no sense (Proverbs 12:11 New International Version).

I know this seems like it should go without saying, but you can't have financial discipline if you don't have any finances. In 2 Thessalonians 3:10 (Berean Study Bible) it says "Even while we were with you, we gave you this command: 'If anyone is unwilling to work, he shall not eat.'" I understand that there are times and things that are out of our control when it comes to work. I've been let go of jobs before because of downsizing which had nothing to do with my work performance. People also get injured on the job or have to move or have other extenuating life circumstances. Notice that the verse above says "If anyone is unwilling to work." It does not say "The one who is not able to work." This verse implies that the person is able to work but not willing. Some advice my dad shared with me about this when I was looking for work was "Until you have a job, your job is finding a job." That meant if you worked 40 hours a week, then you should be putting in 40 hours a week looking for work. Understand that a man without a job lacks purpose, and lack of purpose is a heavy weight to bear.

Work Hard

All hard work brings a profit, but mere talk leads only to poverty (Proverbs 14:23 New International Version).

This one too I wish went without saying. Sadly it doesn't. Your work ethic speaks to your character and integrity. In many ways it is your witness for Jesus to the world around you. Do I work hard when no one is watching or am I the kind of guy who just talks a good game? And, Parents, don't be afraid to push your kids to work. It will be a struggle in the beginning for sure, but it does amazing things for your children's sense of competence and confidence.

Our kids one summer some years ago came to us wanting to go to this camp and that camp and to play on this league and that league. I'm sure any of you with kids can relate to what I'm saying. Assessing our financial picture at the time we could afford it, but it was going to make a dent. Now mind you I want to provide my kids with a good life, but honestly this frustrated me and I called a family meeting to discuss how much all of this was going to cost. I then asked our kids what they thought they could do to make some money to put towards these things they wanted to do. We were able to come up with a flyer with a list of jobs and prices. My daughter was too young at the time, but my boys went around the neighborhood knocking on doors and drumming up business. They were excited to get the jobs but doing them was another story. It took Jaime and I prodding and pushing and definitely some yelling to get the work done. We also worked side by side with them at times to model to them how to work. My boys got into quite a few fights with one another for the first couple of years, but they have been able to grow through it and have become some pretty productive workers. The business has grown to snow removal in the winters as well. No longer do we have to yell and scream at them to get the work done (well we do have to do some reminding, they are kids after all). They have regular clients and sometimes too much work lined up. Our discussions now are not about getting the jobs done, they are about the need to hire other kids to help them get the work done. Our daughter is now in on it too. They are filled with a sense of pride and accomplishment when they finish the jobs and get paid. They now bid their own work and directly interact with many of their customers. So parents, don't be afraid to help your kids in this area of hard work. They will reap the benefit the rest of their lives.

Tithe

Honor the Lord with your wealth and with the best part of everything you produce (Proverbs 3:9 New Living Translation).

Many of you reading this know what a tithe is. If not, it is the practice of giving the first 10 percent of your earnings to God. Most Christians who do this give to their church or a missionary agency or an organization that is helping others. There has been some argument in church circles and amongst people I've talked to as to why we need to do it. "It's an Old Testament thing." "God doesn't need my money." "The church nowadays is only after my money." I'm sure you may have heard some similar things to this as well.

The reality is that tithing is talked about quite a bit in God's playbook, but the question is why? Why is it important? Why does He want us to do it?

To me the tithe speaks to our financial discipline, because it addresses who we honor, as addressed in the verse above. To honor means to regard with great respect. The tithe helps me to honor God first. Our money represents for most of us how we spend the majority of our time. I'm not independently wealthy, so I spend most of my waking hours working to provide for my family. The tithe helps me to keep in perspective where my job, my abilities, my wealth and my stuff comes from. Without it, our sin nature points us back to our own pride. "I did this. I made this money. I deserve this." And with that mindset we will always serve money first.

Save

Take a lesson from the ants, you lazybones. Learn from their ways and become wise! Though they have no prince or governor or ruler to make them work, they labor hard all summer, gathering food for the winter (Proverbs 6:6-8 New Living Translation).

Wealth from get-rich-quick schemes quickly disappears; wealth from hard work grows over time (Proverbs 13:11 New Living Translation).

We already addressed working hard, so the "lazybones" part of these verses is not what I want to discuss. Looking at this example from creation in verse 8 it speaks about how ants gather food for the winter. Yes they work hard all summer, however if they ate all the food in the summer that they gathered, they would starve when winter came. The ants have to save for the hard season ahead. Saving is a hard one for me. My parents tried to instill the practice into me when I was first working, but it seems like there is always something that comes up or something I want that speaks louder.

A couple things I keep in mind for myself with this one. First, I try to think of it like food. For me if it's in front of me I'm going to eat it, so I have to try and keep a lot of junk food out of my house in order to stay healthy. It's the same for me with buying stuff and spending. Advertisers are paid to make you think you need what they are selling. The more time we spend looking, the more convinced we become and the more we spend. It's sort of that "out of sight, out of mind" principle. In essence after tithing, I need to put money away for saving. If it's not in my account (out of sight), then for me it decreases the temptation (out of mind) that I'm going to spend it. I'm not against buying stuff, but save first and be careful to not spend more than you can afford.

The second thing I keep in mind is that I am not going to be able to work forever. There will come a time when my body and mind won't be able to work, so I have to store away for that season. In short, I need to save for retirement. Even just a little out of every paycheck can go a long way if you start early, but you have to put it away first or you'll find a way to spend it.

Live Within Your Means

One person pretends to be rich, yet has nothing; another pretends to be poor, yet has great wealth (Proverbs 13:7 New International Version).

The lesson in this verse seems even more real in this day and age of social media and posting every new purchase you've made or vacation you've been on. "Keeping up with the Joneses" seems a lot more in your face. Comparing your life or your house or your stuff with someone else will only make you feel miserable. There is always someone who has more and always someone who will fake like they have more. I remember having a conversation once with an intern at my job, who came from a certain part of California, which has stuck with me. She told me that most of her neighbors and the people she knew we're faking it. They appeared to have money, but they were actually broke. They lived off of borrowing against the possible accrual of equity in their house and by working multiple jobs, many working seven days a week. I'm not saying this to judge, but that lifestyle can definitely be a heavy weight to carry. Living within your means might not be flashy and will probably not get you a ton of "likes" on social media, but you'll have balance and sleep better at night.

Something else to consider in this is that sometimes we have to put in the extra work to increase our means. Like in sports when we had to increase our strength or speed to get better, sometimes we need to push ourselves in our careers and work in order to make more money. I'm not sure what this looks like for you, but sometimes we have to go for that promotion or go back to school or make that investment in order to move forward. Pray about it, put in the work and trust God will help you as you strive.

Be Careful of Debt (Your Own and Taking on Others)

The rich rule over the poor, and the borrower is the slave of the lender (Proverbs 22:7 English Standard Version).

This one I've fell into a few times over the years, mainly when it came to credit card debt. It's a hard lesson, but if you want something, try saving for it. Some debt is hard to get away from like a mortgage or school loans, but that also comes back to living within your means. Don't be house poor (having a mortgage payment that is too high for your monthly income).

Don't agree to guarantee another person's debt or put up security for someone else. If you can't pay it, even your bed will be snatched from under you (Proverbs 22:26-27 New Living Translation).

Don't take on someone else's debt. Helping someone out by being generous and giving them a gift is one thing, but don't get into a contractual agreement concerning their debt.

Don't Make Big Financial Decisions on Your Own

Without counsel, plans go wrong, but with many advisers they succeed (Proverbs 15:22 New Revised Standard Version).

Seek out others who are wiser and more disciplined than you are when it comes to financial decisions. If you are married, then make sure you are also speaking with your spouse when it comes to the bigger purchases in your life and actually a lot of the smaller purchases too. I'm a big believer in transparency when it comes to financial decisions. It helps keep everyone accountable.

113

Don't Go Grocery Shopping on an Empty Stomach

The plans of the diligent lead surely to abundance, but everyone who is hasty comes only to poverty (Proverbs 21:5 English Standard Version).

The wise have wealth and luxury, but fools spend whatever they get (Proverbs 21:20 New Living Translation).

We all know what I'm talking about here. I'm pretty sure we've all been there before when you're starving and go grocery shopping. You've got a list of food items you need for the week and a budget for those items, but that all goes out the window once you get in the store. Because you're hungry, everything starts to look good, and you start throwing anything and everything into your cart. You quickly and easily convince yourself you need this or that and end up spending twice the amount when you get to the cashier. Be careful of hasty spending decisions when you are totally convinced you have to have this or that thing right now.

Be Generous

A generous person will prosper; whoever refreshes others will be refreshed (Proverbs 11:25 New International Version).

A surefire way to help us not serve money is to use it to help others. Money, like nothing else, typically makes us look at ourselves in a selfish way. What can I get? What's the next thing I want? It is often a never ending cycle which ends in an accumulation of stuff that produces a never ending feeling of dissatisfaction. God's design is for us to use what He has blessed us with to bless others. So use your time, resources and finances to help others.

Integrity

Dishonest scales are an abomination to the Lord, but a just weight is His delight (Proverbs 11:1 New King James Version).

This verse has some strong language in it. The word abomination is not one that gets thrown around lightly in the Bible. God uses it when He is strongly trying to tell us to stay away from something or to intentionally avoid something. Dishonest scales represent unjust or unfair business practices (cheating a customer, cheating on your taxes, not paying your taxes, fixing the books, etc.). These kinds of practices are detestable to God. Often the issue I see with this is that people get away with it enough that the devil tricks them into making it a habit. "As long as I fly under the radar." "Everybody is doing it." "It's a smart move business wise." "No one will ever find out." The issue is that you will reap what you sow. You may get away with it this time or this month or this year, but it will come back to haunt you. I know it is hard, especially when you see the wicked prosper, but "a just weight is His delight." It is always better to live in God's delight.

A Critical and Complaining Spirit

This is another weight we feel entitled to and often times don't understand its destructive nature. As a leader, manager, father, husband or coach I have had to make decisions which weren't very popular at times. I know those people in my life affected by those decisions spoke negatively behind my back and some to my face. I sometimes listened and sometimes got defensive. Sometimes I got it right, and sometimes I definitely didn't. A guiding principle that I have tried to use is to always listen to others' opinions and try to be sure they feel heard by me. I take into account what they are saying and analyze their opinion. I also ask myself, "Has this person ever been in my shoes before? Are they giving me advice from something they learned before from experience in this position?" If they have never done what I am doing when it comes to their feedback, I take that into account. I don't discard their opinion, but I tend to take it with a grain of salt. I also try to apply that to others when I feel entitled to complain about them. It's not to say that I don't have my rant sessions at times where I think I know what to do best in any given situation or complain about my managers at work. I do it and need to repent for my actions and attitude. What I try to do before becoming critical is to ask if I have ever done what that person is doing? Have I been in their position before? If not I really need to be cautious as to what I say. If I have, are my views and feedback coming from a place to help this person or to criticize and complain?

If you have ever coached a team, then you will know that a critical and complaining spirit from the players and parents is one of the most difficult things to address. Everyone is happy and patting you on the back when you are winning, and then everyone is talking trash behind your back when you're not. When that spirit is on your team it is extremely hard to build team cohesiveness and keep players motivated. Parents who have never coached anything in their whole life will freely tell you what you are doing wrong and what you should be doing differently.

God understands this, and it may be why He speaks so strongly about complainers in His word. In the Old Testament, the Israelites were never meant to wander in the wilderness for 40 years before entering into the Promised Land. In Deuteronomy 1:2-3 (New Living Translation) it says "Normally it takes only eleven days to travel from Mount Sinai to Kadesh-barnea, going by way of Mount Seir. But forty years after the Israelites left Egypt, on the first day of the eleventh month, Moses addressed the people of Israel, telling them everything the Lord had commanded him to say." The Israelites turned an 11 day walk into a 40 year death march. It took them 1327 times longer than it was supposed to in order to get to the Promised Land. Why? How did this happen? They had a complaining spirit.

To elaborate on this a bit further in Numbers 14 Moses has to plead with God to not wipe out the Israelites because of their complaining. Numbers 14:11 (New King James Version) says "Then the Lord said to Moses: 'How long will these people reject Me? And how long will they not believe Me, with all the signs which I have performed among them? I will strike with the pestilence and disinherit them, and I will make you a nation greater and mightier than they.'" After this statement, Moses begs God to reconsider, and God does. Two things stand out in verse 11 in terms of how God is affected by the complaining of His people. He sees it as rejection and unbelief. God is not willing to break His covenant with Moses, but tells him that He will give him a new team, a better team ("a nation greater and mightier than they"). Moses intercedes and tells God not to do this, and he can work with the team he's got.

If we skip ahead a few verses it goes on in Numbers 14:20-25 and says "Then the Lord said: 'I have pardoned, according to your word; but truly, as I live, all the earth shall be filled with the glory of the Lord- because all these men who have seen My glory and the signs which I did in Egypt and in the wilderness, and have put Me to the test now these ten times, and have not heeded My voice, they shall certainly not see the land of which I swore to their fathers, nor shall any of those who rejected Me see it. But My servant Caleb, because he has a different spirit in him and has followed Me fully, I will bring into the land where he went, and his descendants shall inherit it. Now the Amalekites and the Canaanites dwell in the valley; tomorrow turn and move out into the wilderness by the Way of the Red Sea.'"

Caleb and Joshua and 10 other spies had gotten back from scouting out the Promised Land that God wanted to give His people. Caleb and Joshua believed they could take the land, but the 10 other spies did not believe and turned the hearts of the people, so they rejected God's promise.

Moses reminds me of a coach who has a team of 12 players. Throughout the regular season, they have prepared and played in some pretty tough games. Against all odds, they have won a lot of the games they should have lost. They even defeated the reigning superpower, the Egyptians. Now they are getting ready to play in the championship game, and instead of remembering all they had been through together and the victories they've had, they see their opponent and are filled with doubt, grumbling and complaint. Moses has two players though, Caleb and Joshua, who still think they can win the game, but that's it. The rest of the team has lost heart. God knows it. Moses knows it. They play that final game and get whipped badly, and that starts the 40 year process and the team rebuild around its two star players, Caleb and Joshua (Numbers 14:26-45).

This scene in the book of Numbers reminds me of a scene in the basketball movie classic *Hoosiers*. In the movie Coach Norman Dale has successfully taken his small rural Indiana high school basketball team, amidst a lot of struggle and community complaints and criticisms, all the way to the state championship. When his team enters the gymnasium in Indianapolis their eyes are wide and their jaws are dropped open in shock as they look around at the sheer size of the building. None of those guys has ever played in an arena of this size before. Coach Dale has anticipated their reaction and calls his team to gather together under the hoop. He then pulls out a tape measure and asks one of his players to hold the one end under the backboard. He walks back to the foul line and asks the player to read out the measurement. The player says "Fifteen feet." Next the coach has a player get on the shoulders of another player and put the tape measure on the rim of the basketball hoop. They read out the measurement, "Ten feet." Coach Dale then says "I think you'll find these exact same measurements as our gym back in Hickory." The team smiles and laughs and then are instructed to get dressed for practice (Pizzo & DeHaven, 1986, 1:34:00).

You see the issue with the spies is that they saw the inhabitants of the Promised Land in Numbers 13 and got scared. They lost faith. They started to complain. In Numbers 13:31 (New King James Version), after Caleb tells the people in the preceding verse they can win this battle, the spies report "We are not able to go against the people, for they are stronger than we." They continue in Numbers 13:33 saying "There we saw the giants (the descendants of Anak came from the giants); and we were like grasshoppers in our own sight, and so we were in their sight." That last sentence is telling, because it is so important in our process of shedding a critical and complaining spirit. "We were like grasshoppers in our own sight, and so we were in their sight." They started to see themselves as small and unable to win and consequently so did their opponents. Understand that their opponents didn't see them this way until they saw themselves this way.

Coach Dale saw this in his players when they entered that gym and got out the tape measure in order to show them that they've seen this battlefield before. His team remembered that and didn't lose heart. In the movie they go on to win the state title. The Israelites chose *not* to remember all that God had done for them, and they lose their battle. The Israelites rejected the Coach and His plan and stopped believing. This is the result of a critical and complaining spirit.

So what do we do to rid ourselves of that weight in our race?

In the world of psychology in the area of Habit Reversal Therapy there is a concept called a "Competing Response." A competing response is a behavior that is incompatible with the habit behavior you are trying to stop. For example when training someone to stop biting their nails you would have the patient become aware when an urge arises to bite their nails and have them hold an object (i.e. a pencil or a toy) in their hand until the urge passes. It is very difficult for them to bite their nails when their hand is closed around an object. The same goes for getting rid of the habit of a complaining spirit.

So what is the competing response we need when we have the urge to criticize and complain?

It's easy for us in hindsight to read the story of the Israelites in the wilderness and look down on them. How could they not believe and trust in God after all He did for them? Why did they complain so much when they got to see miracle after miracle? Like most things it's easier to look at someone else's issues or sin patterns, then to take a look at our own. The issue I find with myself is that I'm not even aware of how often I complain. Complaining and being critical of others has become so commonplace for so many of us, I'm not sure we even know how often we do it.

Has it become habitual? Has it become like biting my nails? Do I not even realize when I'm complaining?

In an article entitled "How Complaining Rewires Your Brain for Negativity" by Travis Bradberry, PhD he discusses how the neurons in our brains rewire when we complain. They rewire in a way that makes it easier for us to repeat the behavior to the point where we don't realize we are doing it. He says "Over time, you find it's easier to be negative than to be positive, regardless of what's happening around you. Complaining becomes your default behavior, which changes how people perceive you." Dr. Bradberry goes on to talk about how complaining can shrink the hippocampus (an area of the brain that deals with problem solving and intelligence) as well and also releases the stress hormone cortisol which can impair our immune system, making us more susceptible to conditions such as high cholesterol, diabetes, heart disease, obesity and make us more vulnerable to strokes. This is pretty alarming stuff, but it doesn't stop there. He goes on to say that since we are inherently social beings, "our brains naturally and unconsciously mimic the moods of those around us." A process called *neuronal mirroring*. Due to this Dr. Bradberry warns "You need to be cautious about spending time with people who complain about everything. Complainers want people to join their pity party, so that they can feel better about themselves (Bradberry, T., n.d.)."

These two factors are what was going on with the Israelites and the spies that Moses sent out. They had been complaining so much it seems that they got to the point where it was easier to be negative than to be positive, regardless of what was happening around them. Regardless of all the miracles God had done and the ways He had taken care of them and interceded for them, they had rewired their brains to the point where complaining became their default behavior. They had also mimicked the moods of those around them, reinforcing this negative behavior which God needed to address.

Dr. Bradberry's article goes on to say we need to "cultivate an attitude of gratitude." When we want to complain we shift our attention to being grateful for something.

Gratitude is the competing response to reverse the habit of a critical and complaining spirit.

I can't be grateful and complaining at the same time. If the Israelites would have been grateful for all God had done for them, their trip to the Promised Land would've been a whole lot shorter. We have to practice gratefulness, just like anything else we want to get better at. A psychiatrist I used to work with would ask his patients if they were able to clean themselves after using the bathroom. With an alarmed look on their faces, they would answer yes. His response to them would be "Then you always have something to be thankful for. There are many people who can't."

I try to pray when I wake up and when I go to bed each day thanking God for the day. I don't do it because I like to. I do it because I want to rewire my brain for being positive, and I do that by remembering the good. I ask my kids every night when we pray before they go to bed to tell God one thing they are thankful for that day. It sometimes mystifies me how long it will take them to think of one thing to say, but that is us as humans isn't it? We so quickly forget. The Bible uses the word remember over and over again (actually over 250 times), because we need to wire our brains towards remembering the good. We don't need any help in recalling the negative or complaining.

The article goes on to state as well that thinking about what you are grateful for reduces your stress hormone cortisol by 23% which improves mood, energy and decreases anxiety. He also says that if you are going to complain (which we will all do at times) that we need to engage in "Solution-Oriented Complaining" (complaining with a purpose). He says "Before complaining, know what outcome you're looking for. If you can't identify a purpose, there's a good chance you just want to complain for its own sake, and that's the kind of complaining you should nip in the bud (Bradberry, T., n.d.)"

Lastly, with the process of *neuronal mirroring* in mind, we need to surround ourselves with more *Joshuas* and *Calebs*. Since we tend to mimic the moods of those around us, we need to put ourselves around people who are hopeful, positive, resourceful, motivated, faith-filled, and solution-oriented. These are the kind of people you want on your team, so that you can be a more transformative influence on the world around you.

Anxiety/Fear/Worry

It is common practice in my clinic to screen every patient on almost every visit for depression and anxiety symptoms. I often get the question from people who are suffering from the symptoms of anxiety, "So what is anxiety anyway?" People recognize the symptoms and the discomfort and disruption it brings to their life but have a hard time putting their finger on exactly what it is. Sometimes it's easy for some to name a specific fear, but many times people have trouble with identifying things that are causing them to experience anxiety. When asked the question "What is making you anxious?" patients will often answer "I don't know exactly. Everything!" Anxiety is like that. If affects us physically, mentally, behaviorally, emotionally, relationally and spiritually. It's hard to nail down sometimes. For those who suffer from anxiety it can be a very debilitating condition. Proverbs 12:25 (English Standard Version) says "Anxiety in a man's heart weighs him down, but a good word makes him glad." According to an article in the journal *Dialogues in Clinical Neuroscience* in 2015 anxiety disorders are the most prevalent mental disorders, affecting up to 33.7% of the population sometime during their lifetime (Bandelow & Michaelis, 2015, p. 327).

So why are anxiety rates so high?

This is a tough question to answer, and there are a lot of theories out there. An article entitled "Anxiety in the West: Is it on the rise?" in Medical News Today posits some theories. In the article the author looks at anxiety rates in the U.S. and discusses that the increase in materialism, loneliness, societal stress, the use of social media and even the chemicals we are exposed to could all be factors that are driving these increases. For example he cites a study done in the 1990s that "found that people who pursued money, looks and status were more likely to feel anxious and depressed." This was in the 1990s! I would say the importance of money, looks and status have grown quite a bit since then. The introduction of social media has also definitely reinforced those values. In fact the article also cites an investigation of 1700 young U.S. adults and found that "people who frequented higher numbers of social platforms reported higher levels of depression and anxiety." None of these factors are causal but they could be playing a role and shouldn't be dismissed. He concludes with the following:

"Perhaps anxiety is prevalent in the U.S. because of all or none of the above. After all, everyone is different, and anxiety may have a myriad of causes in each individual.

Unraveling the ins and outs of mental health is not a simple task; conditions overlap, symptoms vary, and cause and effect are blurred.

Is anxiety a spectrum that we all inhabit? Is humanity a naturally anxious species? Its severity and prevalence might fluctuate with the social conditions of the time, but perhaps it is within us all. (Newman, 2018)."

To be clear anxiety or fear or worry is not something you can just get rid of or take off like a dirty shirt. There are real things that happen to real people that cause these disorders. Some people are predisposed through no fault of their own. Some people are abused and see and experience things they should never have to witness or go through. I listen to these stories everyday while at work. I try to encourage and pray and give hope to some very broken lives. I agree with the author's statement above that "unraveling the ins and outs of mental health is not a simple task."

So what do we do? Are we doomed to live under this weight? Does God's word have anything to say about it?

Well the Bible actually commands us to not be anxious (Philippians 4:6), to not worry (Matthew 6:25) and to not fear (Isaiah 41:10). In fact the Bible tells us in some form or other to "not be afraid" or "to fear not" or "to not worry" or "to not be anxious" or "to not be discouraged" many times throughout the scripture. So my next question is this:

If the Bible is telling me over and over to not be afraid or anxious, is my anxiety a sin?

I met with a patient once who told me she had been extremely stressed out over the past year. Her anxiety symptom screener reflected that. I asked her about what was going on, and she went on to tell me about her financial worries, her worries for her kids, her worries about her health and her worries about her marriage. Her anxiety was crippling her life. The next thing she said caught my attention. She told me she was a Christian and that she goes to church, but she felt she couldn't go talk to anyone in her church about what was going on in her life. I asked her why, and she responded that "They would tell me that I just needed more faith." That started a conversation between us in which I asked her if she thought her anxious feelings were sinful. She wasn't sure how to answer that. I then asked her if she thought Jesus was a sinner. She answered that, and said Jesus never sinned. From there we began to look at what Jesus was going through in the Garden of Gethsemane the night before he was to be crucified. In Luke 22:41-44 (New King James Version) it says:

> And He was withdrawn from them about a stone's throw, and He knelt down and prayed, saying "Father, if it is Your will, take this cup away from Me; nevertheless not My will, but Yours, be done." Then an angel appeared to Him from heaven, strengthening Him. And being in agony, He prayed more earnestly. Then His sweat became like great drops of blood falling to the ground.

Jesus was experiencing what is called hematidrosis, which is a very rare medical condition that causes one to sweat blood from your skin when you haven't been cut. It is believed to be related to your body's "fight or flight" response and is caused by extreme distress or fear (https://www.webmd.com/a-to-z-guides/hematidrosis-hematohidrosis#1). Our "fight or flight" response is our built-in reaction to anxiety. So Jesus was having an extreme level of anxiety the night before He was to be crucified, and rightfully so.

I say all this to debunk the myth that if we feel anxious or afraid or worried, then we are in sin. I often tell my patients that we don't want to *not* have any anxiety at all or we would just walk out in traffic on a busy street and be killed or seriously hurt. It is a God-given protective measure. *Feeling* anxiety or fear or worry is not a sin. Feelings are natural (part of being human), neutral (neither good nor bad) and normal (they happen to everyone).

So where does that leave us? If Jesus feels anxiety and so do we, then why are we commanded to not be anxious?

I am going to answer that question with another question. If I *feel* something, do I have to *be* that thing? I am not commanded *to not feel* anxiety. I am commanded *to not become* anxiety. The same would go for anger. I can get angry and not become my anger. Jesus got angry and did not sin (John 2:14-17).

Let's dissect Jesus' response to his anxiety in the verses above in Luke 22 and also the same account in the Gospel of Mark. Jesus was facing an intense anxiety producing situation. He was about to be betrayed by his friends, beaten, mocked, crucified and separated from God. We have no earthly idea the amount of stress he was under during that time. He knew the trial and pain that was coming, so how did He respond?

1. **Get Support**- In Mark's account of this incident in Mark 14:32-33 (New King James Version) it says "Then they came to a place which was named Gethsemane; and He said to His disciples, 'Sit here while I pray.' And He took Peter, James and John with Him, and He began to be troubled and deeply distressed."

    Jesus got his team together with Him in His time of deep distress. He didn't isolate himself. I wrote earlier about one of the possible factors leading to a rise in anxiety rates in the U.S. is loneliness. The devil loves to use that one on us, getting our mental tapes to run and saying things like "I'm all alone." "Nobody likes me." "Nobody understands me." One of the most common things I see with my anxious or depressed patients are people who are isolated, and in therapy we have to begin the work of building their support system. So the first thing I see in Jesus response to feelings of anxiety, fear and worry is that He got His team together. "He took Peter, James and John with Him."

2. **Pray-** In Mark 14:35 it says "He went a little farther, and fell on the ground, and prayed that if it were possible, the hour might pass from Him."

In the previous verse (Mark 14:34) Jesus asks His friends to keep an eye on Him as He went to pray. Honestly that is not my typical reaction when I am in a state of anxiety or worry, and my friends are with me. What I usually do (and I have a feeling I'm not the only one) is complain. I start to tell my friends all of my problems and issues. Jesus doesn't do that. He takes it to His Father in prayer first. Jesus cast His cares on God first. There's a lesson in that for us when it comes to anxiety, fear and worry.

There is a plethora of academic studies and literature out there verifying the positive outcome and benefit of prayer in decreasing anxiety. Just do an internet search with the keywords: "peer reviewed study prayer decreasing anxiety" and do some research yourself. The scientific literature out there proving prayer's benefits is vast.

Also if you think about anxiety symptoms from a physiological perspective, our brains begin to go into panic mode because our heart rate has increased and our breathing gets shallower and more rapid which is causing too much carbon dioxide to build up in our system. A technique to combat this is called controlled breathing which has one focus on the amount of air they are breathing in and out over a period of time in order to get the proper amount of oxygen. Prayer can also be a meditative means to slow us down during those times of anxiety and panic and restore our breathing and oxygen intake.

3. **Call Out to God-** Mark 14:36 goes on to say "And He said, 'Abba Father.'"

Abba Father is an intimate term as one would refer to his or her own "dad." It's like those times when you're really struggling with something and you call up your dad and tell him you need to talk. That is what Jesus is doing in this instance. He is not holding it all in, stuffing it down and trying to tough it out. He is pouring out His heart to His Father. God wants us to do the same with Him. He's big enough to handle our problems.

Your relationship with someone deepens when you feel safe to let them know what's going on with you. There is some faulty thinking that goes on in some people's relationship with God in which they don't feel they can to talk to Him about their problems, worries or fears. They say things like "God doesn't have time for my little problems" or "So many people have it so much worse than I do." The devil uses these thoughts to keep us separated from the Father, and that is not what Jesus modeled to us when He experienced anxiety. Matthew 11:28 (New International Version) says "Come to me, all you who are weary and burdened, and I will give you rest." The words weary and burdened can be synonymous with stress or worry. Jesus is instructing us to come to Him when we are in that state in order to get rest and peace. He is not saying suck it up and deal with it on our own.

4. **Process the Feeling-** The rest of the verse in Mark 14:36 (New King James Version) Jesus goes on to say "all things are possible for You. Take this cup away from Me; nevertheless, not what I will, but what You will."

Jesus is processing the feelings and decisions He has in front of Him. Often times when we don't audibly speak out our anxious thoughts they become like a hamster wheel that goes around and around, something called racing thoughts. There is a book I often use with my patients who are struggling with anxiety called *Mind Over Mood*. There is an exercise/worksheet in the book called a "Thought Record" in which a person analyzes their moods and thoughts in order to address and challenge their thinking. The worksheet follows a process of:

1. Identifying the Situation

2. Identifying and Rating your mood (0-100%)

3. Identifying Automatic Thoughts (related to the situation you are experiencing)

4. Identifying evidence that supports your automatic thought

5. Identifying evidence that does not support your automatic thought

6. Coming up with an alternative/balanced thought

7. Rerating your mood (Greenberger and Padesky, 1995, p. 34-35)

Let's look at this process as it relates to Jesus in the Garden of Gethsemane:

Jesus is in the Garden of Gethsemane with His disciples praying the night before He was to be crucified. Given that Jesus is in a state of anguish to where He is sweating blood we could safely say He is feeling Anxiety at 100% and Fear at 100%. He knows He is going to be betrayed, beaten, crucified and separated from the Father. Jesus is praying and says to God "all things are possible for You." He is going through His mind and saying that God can take this away from Him. He can stop it. He can save Him from the pain ahead. Because of this He goes on to say "Take this cup away from Me," but then he takes a turn in His thinking. Jesus recognizes God has a plan for His life and that His Father is trustworthy. He analyzes the evidence and concludes that God's way is best in spite of the anxiety He feels. He then says "nevertheless, not what I will, but what You will." Like Jesus we have to view our situations in the light of who God is and what He says. We have to weigh the evidence of His word and His trustworthiness in our lives in order to produce an alternative and balanced thought when we feel anxiety, worry and fear.

5. **Strengthen Your Spirit-** In Luke's account in Luke 22:42-43 (New King James Version) it says "Father, if it is Your will, take this cup away from me; nevertheless not my will, but Yours be done." Then an angel appeared to Him from heaven, strengthening Him.

Jesus sought heavenly strength to face what was ahead. He was struggling in his humanity to face what was in front of Him to do. He looked to a higher source for comfort.

I mentioned earlier about the patient who said she couldn't go talk to anyone in her church about her stress, because they would just tell her she needed more faith. It is unfortunate for her, and I don't know her church situation. However the reality is that it does take faith to face the stresses and difficulties of this life.

So how do we have faith to strengthen our spirits as Jesus did? In Romans 10:17 (New King James Version) it says "So then faith comes by hearing, and hearing by the word of God." If our faith comes from hearing the word of God as the verse tells us, then do we know the word of God when we need it? Do we know it so we can strengthen our spirits with it? I often times will be in session with a person who professes to be a Christian, and we will start to discuss what God's word says about his or her particular struggle. I'll start reciting a verse or section of scripture, and the person will finish the sentence for me. I'll say another verse, and the patient will again finish my sentence. You can see the lightbulb go on as they start to connect what the word of God is saying in relation to the struggle they are having.

I referenced an article earlier in this chapter entitled "How Complaining Rewires Your Brain for Negativity." I want to reiterate a point from that article by quoting the first paragraph:

"Your brain loves efficiency and doesn't like to work any harder than it has to. When you repeat a behavior, such as complaining, your neurons branch out to each other to ease the flow of information. This makes it much easier to repeat that behavior in the future- so easy, in fact, that you might not even realize you're doing it. (Bradberry, T., n.d.)."

What the author is referring to is known as the neuroplasticity of our brain. Science is coming to realize more and more that we have the power to change the wiring of our brains. In essence what we think about and do we become, which we have discussed a bit earlier in the book. I talk to my patients about how they have repeated thoughts and behaviors so much that they have basically built an eight lane super highway in their brain with their neurons. The information and reactions travel so quickly across that they don't have time to react differently than they've always done. The article above talked about complaining in this regard, but what if we substituted anxiety for complaining. Our reactions to the feelings of anxiety, fear or worry have been repeated so much "you might not even realize you're doing it." I then talk to them about needing to start the process of building another "road" in their brains. This is the work of Romans 12:2 (New International Version) where it says "Do not conform to the pattern of this world, but be transformed by the renewing of your mind. Then you will be able to test and approve what God's will is- his good, pleasing and perfect will." The renewing of our mind is the process of thinking as God wants us to think. Jesus tested and approved God's will for Him in the Garden of Gethsemane as He processed His feelings. He was scared to do what was in front of Him, but he renewed His mind and strengthened His spirit.

God calls us to keep His word on our lips and meditate on it day and night (Joshua 1:8). In the world of psychotherapy this practice would be known as a form of mindfulness. Being mindful and aware of what God is telling us. It is through this mindfulness of God that we build new pathways in our brains. In Psalm 16: 8-9 (New Revised Standard Version) David writes "I keep the Lord always before me; because he is at my right hand, I shall not be moved. Therefore my heart is glad, and my soul rejoices; my body also rests secure."

6. **Face It-** The account in Mark 14:41-42 (The Message) goes on to say "Time's up. The Son of Man is about to be betrayed into the hands of sinners. Get up. Let's get going. My betrayer has arrived."

In this passage Jesus has to wake up His friends who repeatedly fell asleep on Him as He was going through the hardest moment of His life. I guess it's good to know we're not alone when we feel like our friends and family are sometimes not there for us in our hardest times. In any case how does Jesus react? Does He run off? Does He try to escape? No, He faces His betrayer. He faces His anxiety.

When I meet with my patients and we discuss anxiety, one of the things I tell them is that if you leave anxiety alone it won't stay stagnant. It doesn't stay the same. It gets bigger. If you don't confront it, it will grow. In an article entitled "11 Ways Your Brain Changes When You Don't Treat Your Anxiety" the author outlines a number of issues that arise when we don't face our anxiety, some of which include difficulty concentrating, forgetting how to calm down, developing other mental health issues, insomnia, staying stuck on "high alert," cellular malfunction, fears reinforcing themselves, parts of your brain shrinking, and a decreased immune system (Steber, C., 2018).

In psychotherapy, treatment for anxiety involves exposure to what is causing the patient to be anxious through a process called systematic desensitization (which is what I like to refer as going "little by little" through exposing the patient to more anxiety producing stimuli and practicing ways to decrease their anxiety response) or flooding (exposing the patient to the most anxiety-producing stimuli right away). Jesus would have went through more of the "flooding" type of treatment as depicted in the verses above.

Facing one's anxieties, worries and fears is no easy task. The first thing we have to remember and go back to is that we are not alone in this process. In Psalm 55:22 (Contemporary English Version) it says "Our Lord, we belong to you. We tell you what worries us, and you won't let us fall." We have to recognize that God has us. We belong to Him. From that place we can proclaim Hebrews 13:6 (English Standard Version) where it says "So we can confidently say, 'The Lord is my helper; I will not fear; what can man do to me?'" Our confidence is in Him. We may change or waver, but He does not, and through His strength He is calling us to be like Him.

The Bible is full of story after story of people who faced their anxieties with God's help. Think of Moses, Noah, Joshua, Esther, David, the prophets, the disciples, Paul, and so on. Their stories and examples are there for us to build our faith in the face of our fear, so that we can as it says in Joshua 1:9 (New King James Version) "Be strong and of good courage; do not be afraid, nor be dismayed, for the Lord your God is with you wherever you go." The end of that verse is a key concept where it says "God is with you wherever you go." It presupposes that we will "go." In order to not become our feelings of anxiety, worry and fear we have to go and face them. This is how we renew our minds in building new roads with our thoughts that are not from a "spirit of fear, but of power and of love and of a sound mind (2 Timothy 1:7)."

Approval of Man

Everyone has a need for approval inside of them. We might not care about everyone's opinions about us, and some may care about it more than others, however to think to yourself that you don't care about anyone's approval of you would be foolish.

Do you care what your boss thinks of you? Do you care what your spouse thinks of you? Do you care what your parents think of you? How about your close friends? Or your neighbors?

If I want to keep my job, do well at my job and possibly advance in my job, then I better care what my boss thinks of me. I should be aware of the level of my work ethic and production. If I want to have a good marriage, then I should be aware of my spouse's opinions on how things are going and what I may need to do differently. The same should go for the close friends I put on my "team." God calls us to honor our parents (Exodus 20:12) and to love our neighbor (Mark 12:31). Another angle on this is as an athlete if you wanted to play on the team, then you needed to care what your coach thought of you.

So if we are to be concerned about what others think of us to some degree, then where does this become a weight that slows us down? Realize there is a difference between being concerned or aware of what those close to you or those who are placed in authority over you think of you and going to those people for recognition, validation and approval. I'll explain. We all have a "God-shaped hole" that we try to fill with something (accomplishments, food, sex, experiences, money, relationships, etc.), and some of us try to fill that hole with the approval of others. I have filled that hole with many things over the years and even today have to fairly often question myself in my daily life as to what I am filling it with besides Jesus. So yes I am saying that even Christians who have accepted Jesus' love for them will struggle with the weight of wanting man's approval.

If that is the case, then how do we address this in our lives?

As a child we feel loved when we feel approval. It starts really young, and it's quite hard to split the difference in our minds between love and approval at that age. If I do something right as a child, and my parents notice me and praise me (approval), then I feel reinforced. I feel good. That feeling of reinforcement can become synonymous in my mind with the concept of love. Conversely if I do something wrong and get in trouble (disapproval), then I think my parents don't love me anymore. I feel bad. I know this is simplified in its approach, but I think it will help drive home the point as we move forward.

The problem is that if we continue in this mindset, then we become stuck in a pattern where we constantly need the approval or reinforcement of others in order to feel loved. If I don't get that approval, then I am unloved and see myself as unloved. And that is a very big weight to bear. A lot of unhealthy and sinful behaviors and mindsets will follow suit. This is where the gospel of Jesus is either a freedom or a stumbling block for a lot of people when they come to this crossroad.

In Ephesians 2:8-9 (New King James Version) it says "For by grace you have been saved through faith, and that not of yourselves; it is the gift of God, not of works, lest anyone should boast." Christianity is the only religion where God, in the form of His Son Jesus, came down to man and paid the price for the wrongs we have done. All other religions require us to ascend towards the divine by means of our own actions. This is true freedom for some and an issue for others who struggle with having someone else paying their debt. Even the early Christian church struggled with this concept of mixing their own good works in with God's gift of Jesus as the means of their salvation (Galatians 5). I think it is something we all still struggle with today on some level as well.

In order to separate love and approval, we need to first understand that there is nothing we can do to make God love us any more or any less. We can't earn His love. It's free (Romans 5:8). You don't have to believe in Him or you could hate God, and that still won't change. There is also nothing that we can do to separate us from His love. In Romans 8:38-39 (New International Version) Paul writes "For I am convinced that neither death nor life, neither angels nor demons, neither the present nor the future, nor any powers, neither height nor depth, nor anything in all creation, will be able to separate us from the love of God that is in Christ Jesus our Lord." So in short we can't earn or lose God's love.

This has to be the starting point in our mind and spirit in order to strip off this weight. If we can truly know and understand God's love for us, then we can begin to love ourselves apart from our shortcomings or our pride. If we can really get a hold of how God sees us and values us, then we can begin to see ourselves in the same way. We can begin to speak over ourselves in the same way that God sees us. Without that we will try and fill that hole with recognition, compliments and approval from others, because let's face it those things feel good. The issue is they don't last, and the hole is still there, so the cycle repeats.

The second step to this is about trust. Do I trust God? Do I trust He will take care of me? Do I trust He will reward me for the good that I do? If the answer is no to any of these questions, then we will seek our approval and recognition from man. We will seek out man's reward to get our needs met.

In Colossians 3:23-24 (New King James Version) it says "And whatever you do, do it heartily, as to the Lord and not to men, knowing that from the Lord you will receive the reward of the inheritance; for you serve the Lord Christ." Let's take a little closer look at this piece of scripture.

"And whatever you do"- That means everything you do (at work, at home, with your spouse, with your friends, with your kids, etc.).

"Do it heartily"- Give it everything you've got.

"As to the Lord and not to men,"- You are working for God, not man.

"From the Lord you will receive the reward"- God will reward you. God will take care of you.

We have to understand that we are working unto God and not man, and that He will take care of us. It may not happen right away or exactly when we want it or how we want it, but He is true to His word. He will come through.

Jesus also had some words for us when it came to addressing our motives for recognition from man. In Matthew 6:1-4 (New King James Version) He says "Take heed that you do not do your charitable deeds before men, to be seen by them. Otherwise you have no reward from your Father in heaven. Therefore, when you do a charitable deed, do not sound a trumpet before you as the hypocrites do in the synagogues and in the streets, that they may have glory from men. Assuredly, I say to you, they have their reward. But when you do a charitable deed, do not let your left hand know what your right hand is doing, that your charitable deed may be done in secret; and your Father who sees in secret will Himself reward you openly."

So to summarize the steps of stripping off the weight of man's approval:

1. **Know**- Know that God loves you. You can't earn it, and you can't lose it.
2. **Work**- Work unto God and not man. Am I doing my best at what God has given me to do?
3. **Check your motives**- Do not do your good deeds to be recognized by man. Am I doing my best at what God has given me to do for Him or so that I may be recognized and approved by others? What gives me validation? Is it the praise and recognition of others? The issue is that God gives us gifts and abilities. We can use those abilities for our own glory or use them to point others to Him.

Remember in Matthew 5:16 (New Living Translation) where it says "In the same way, let your good deeds shine out for all to see, so that everyone will praise your heavenly Father."

4. **Trust**- Trust that God sees what you do and will reward you. We don't need to know God's timing. We need to know He is faithful. Here are some verses that help me during these times of doubt and struggles with trust:

Trust in the Lord with all your heart, And lean not on your own understanding; In all your ways acknowledge Him, And He shall direct your paths (Proverbs 3:5-6 New King James Version).

So be content with who you are, and don't put on airs. God's strong hand is on you; he'll promote you at the right time. Live carefree before God; he is most careful with you (1 Peter 5:6 The Message).

The steps of a good man are ordered by the Lord: and he delighteth in his way. Though he fall, he shall not be utterly cast down: for the Lord upholdeth him with his hand (Psalm 37:23-24 King James Version).

To close out this chapter as we try to "run with endurance the race God has set before us" we need to be prayerfully aware to "strip off every weight that slows us down" and "the sin that so easily trips us up." We need to remain vigilant about who and what we allow on our team. The words of Paul in Romans 8:6 (New Living Translation) pretty clearly outline our choice where it says "So letting your sinful nature control your mind leads to death. But letting the Spirit control your mind leads to life and peace."

PART 4
(HOW)

Chapter 8

<u>How to Fulfill Your Potential</u>

"The quality of a person's life is in direct proportion to their commitment to excellence, regardless of their chosen field of endeavor."

-Vince Lombardi

In my work I am often asked by people who have been hurt, abused, cheated on or abandoned "How do you know when you can trust someone?" We all know from life experiences and relationships that it takes a long time to trust someone but a very short time (often one decision or action) to lose trust in someone.

I often rephrase this question to them stating, "So what you are asking me is how you know when someone is trustworthy? Worthy of your trust?" My answer is simple. In gauging if you can trust someone, ask yourself does this person do what they say and do they do it consistently? Consistently is not once or twice or for a week or a month but over a long period of time. What do you see in the *fruit* of their life from their actions, decisions and behaviors? Anyone can tell you something, but that means nothing until they do it. Doing something consistently, day in and day out, year in and year out is what produces the *good fruit* and trustworthiness in someone's life.

We discussed this next section of scripture earlier in Chapter 6 when analyzing some of the process of choosing a pastor, but let's read it again:

> Beware of false prophets, who come to you in sheep's clothing, but inwardly they are ravenous wolves. You will know them by their fruits. Do men gather grapes from thornbushes or figs from thistles? Even so, every good tree bears good fruit, but a bad tree bears bad fruit. A good tree cannot bear bad fruit, nor can a bad tree bear good fruit. Every tree that does not bear good fruit is cut down and thrown into the fire. Therefore by their fruits you will know them (Matthew 7:15-20 New King James Version).

So to summarize Jesus' words here you will know someone, learn to trust someone, gauge someone by the fruits they produce or the results of their consistent decisions and actions over time. It is one thing to look at and question someone through this lens and another thing to turn the lens on ourselves to examine our own lives.

Am I trustworthy? What is the fruit that I am producing? How do I treat others? What would my spouse or my children or my friends or coworkers say about me if they were asked anonymously?

These are tough questions to ask, but the answers will speak to the fruit of your life. Remember that "the fruit of the Spirit is love, joy, peace, longsuffering, kindness, goodness, faithfulness, gentleness, self-control (Galatians 5:22-23 New King James Version)." A life that is connected to the Spirit of God will reflect those qualities.

So how do I produce good fruit in my life? Another way to ask this is how do I fulfill my potential?

As athletes or people who watch athletics we all know someone who looked good on paper but never really fulfilled their potential. Maybe looking back on your own athletic career you may feel you didn't quite accomplish all that you could have. I know sometimes I do, however bigger than that we don't want to look back on the entirety of our lives and feel that way.

In Chapter 4 when we talked about the qualities of a good coach, we discussed how a good coach pushes you to reach your potential. When we wanted to know how to play our best or get the best results out of whatever sport we were playing we met with the coach who talked to us about what we needed to do in order to get better. They gave us a game plan in order to improve our skill set, our fitness and our mental toughness. They helped us in preparing our bodies as well as our minds, so that we could produce the best results for ourselves and the team.

Our relationship with God is similar to spending time with that coach. God will show us the areas of our life where we need to improve and where we need to grow. This happens through communicating with him in prayer. Talking with Him and listening to Him. This is not just praying to Him when your marriage is falling apart or your girlfriend broke up with you or you just lost your job. This is continual communication. This is consistent communication. I sometimes hear when I talk with people in regards to their communication with God something like "I never hear from God" or "God never speaks to me." I'm not disagreeing with their view on this, but how often are we speaking with Him and making space to hear from Him? God makes a statement about this in Jeremiah 29:13 (New International Version) where He says "You will seek me and find me when you seek me with all your heart." Just imagine as an athlete going to your coach and asking how you could get better at whatever sport or position you are playing and then leaving the office or the field before he or she could give you an answer. It wouldn't do you much good.

In Hebrews 11:6 (New King James Version) it says "But without faith it is impossible to please Him, for he who comes to God must believe that He is, and that He is a rewarder of those who diligently seek Him." The definition of diligence is careful and persistent work or effort. Coming to God once a year when your life is falling apart is okay. God will listen to you and wants to help you, but that is not a relationship in which you are diligently seeking Him and in which He will reward you. In short we can't hear from God if we first don't believe He is God and if we aren't consistently spending time with Him, because we won't recognize His voice (John 10:4).

Hearing God's Voice

In 1 Kings 19 Elijah is running for his life from Jezebel. The interesting thing about that is that in the previous chapter Elijah had just won a huge victory over the prophets of Baal. God ended a three year drought, and Elijah was filled with God's power and outran a horse. Even with all of that supernatural working in his life he runs scared when Jezebel threatens him and wishes God would take his life. God meets Elijah there in his despair as he is hiding in a cave.

In 1 Kings 19:11-13 (New King James Version) it says:

Then He said, "Go out, and stand on the mountain before the Lord." And behold, the Lord passed by, and a great and strong wind tore into the mountains and broke the rocks in pieces before the Lord, but the Lord was not in the wind; and after the wind an earthquake, but the Lord was not in the earthquake; and after the earthquake a fire, but the Lord was not in the fire; and after the fire a still small voice.

So it was, when Elijah heard it, that he wrapped his face in his mantle and went out and stood in the entrance of the cave. Suddenly a voice came to him, and said, "What are you doing here, Elijah?"

It was the "still small voice," not the wind, the earthquake or the fire. God used the wind, earthquake and fire to get Elijah's attention, so he could hear the still small voice. I will tell you that it is hard to hear a still small voice if you are surrounded by distractions and aren't listening pretty intently, and there are a ton of distractions around us in this day and age.

So how do we hear the still small voice? How do we know what God is trying to tell us?

1. Repent

The first thing we need to address that hinders us in our communication with God is what I talked about in Chapter 2 where I lost my focus due to sin. In Isaiah 59:2 (English Standard Version) it says "but your iniquities have made a separation between you and your God, and your sins have hidden his face from you so that he does not hear." We need to address our sin patterns first and repent. Remember from Chapter 4 that a good coach needs to rebuke and correct the team before he or she can train them (2 Timothy 3:16-17). The team cannot be trained until they have responded to the corrections.

Is there sin in my life that is preventing me from hearing from God? Have I heeded God's rebuke and correction, so that He can begin to train me? Are there areas of my flesh, ego and pride I need to address?

2. Deal with Distractions

Every year in January my church has us do a fast for the month. Our pastor challenges us to pick something or some things that we are going to give up or abstain from for the month as we seek God for direction for the year ahead. Honestly I dread it every year. I'm not a good "faster" I guess, but I don't think any of us really are. We are being asked to deny ourselves and deny our flesh which is never fun. Some things I've fasted over the years for example are meat, sweets, bread, alcohol, social media, TV/movies, coffee, eating after 7:00pm, etc. As we are praying about what to fast we are to ask God and ourselves what is getting in the way of us hearing His voice.

Now mind you God wants to speak to you, just as good parents want to speak to and instruct their children in order to help them have successful and healthy lives. So with that in mind He will most likely be pretty direct about what He would like you to fast or helping you to identify what is a distraction in your life which is hindering you from hearing Him. Often the issue on my part is not wanting to give that up.

So during that month of fasting the idea is that we seek Him in prayer and listening each time we crave that thing we are fasting or with the extra time we may now have due to giving up something like social media or TV. It is also a good idea to take notes on your phone or carry a notebook in your car or office or home. As you seek Him and hear from Him write it down. Some years I have heard from Him throughout the month and other years I didn't seem to get direction for the year until the end of the month. On some years the direction was very specific and other years not so much, but I can attest to the fact that I always heard something.

We need to understand that it takes faith as I mentioned earlier (Hebrews 11:6) and "he who comes to God must believe that He is." He is what? That He is God. It doesn't work otherwise. I have to believe that God is God and has a plan for my life. In sports if I went to my coach I needed to believe he had advice that would help me get better. We also have to understand that "…that the natural man does not receive the things of the Spirit of God, for they are foolishness to him; nor can he know them, because they are spiritually discerned." (1 Corinthians 2:14-15 New King James Version). Fasting and praying help us to "spiritually discern." Throughout scripture God wants us to seek Him for guidance, direction and provision through prayer and fasting (Ezra 8:23, Daniel 1:12-17, Esther 4:16 and Acts 13:2-3 are just a few examples).

3. Follow Through

It is one thing to hear a word or be given counsel or advice on something, and it is another thing to do something about it. Remember in James 2:20 (New King James Version) it pretty clearly and bluntly states that "faith without works is dead." In essence the coach can spell out for you what you need to do to become a better player, but nothing will happen unless you go out and do what you are being told. You need to follow through. In all my years of coaching I have always given my players drills and exercises they can do at home to get better, but easily the majority of my players never put in any extra time outside of practice. The ones who do quickly set themselves apart from the rest.

This is the process of becoming personally trustworthy and fulfilling my potential. Do I do what I say and do it consistently? Do I accept God's teaching, rebuking and correcting and then follow through on how He is training me?

Game Plans

The following are some of the specific game plans God has revealed to me throughout the years of seeking Him through prayer and fasting. One year God began speaking to me about my health. I have three children with a five year age span from the oldest to the youngest, so the years before they got into elementary school I worked three jobs (one full-time and two part-time), so Jaime could stay home to raise them. It was important for us to have one of us home during those years. This meant some long days and very minimal sleep for both of us. Unfortunately this also meant my health suffered. At a doctor's appointment I was told my blood pressure was too high and I needed to lose 20 to 30 pounds. This was quite a shock for me, since I always saw myself as an athlete and felt like I kept myself in pretty decent shape. Obviously that wasn't the case anymore.

As I prayed about it God brought to my mind a question that a boss asked me once and one that I share with my patients in therapy today. It goes something like this:

> Have you ever flown in an airplane? Even if you haven't have you ever seen a movie or a TV show where there are people flying on an airplane, and the airline steward has to give a speech before you take off in order to go over safety procedures and what to do in case of an emergency? What does the airline steward instruct you to do if there is a loss in cabin pressure and a mask drops down from the overhead compartment, and you are traveling with children or someone requiring assistance? Do you put the mask on your child or yourself first?

Often times my patients, like myself, when I was asked that question said they would put the mask on the child first. That seems right and rational. You should take care of the child first. Your child would be in a panic and need you to put the mask on in order get oxygen, however this is not what the airline steward instructs us to do. We are told to secure the mask on ourselves first and then secure the mask on our children.

I then ask my patients "Why do you think that is the case?" They think about it for a minute and the light bulb comes on and they say "Because if I don't get the mask on myself and die then I can't take care of my kid." It's a pretty extreme example, but it stuck in my mind and my soul.

If I don't take care of myself how can I take care of anyone else?

As I wrestled with this question God gave me the scripture in which Jesus is being questioned about what is the greatest commandment in Mark 12:28-34 (New International Version). Specifically He pointed me to verse 31 where it says "Love your neighbor as yourself."

The Holy Spirit spoke to me regarding this piece of scripture saying if I don't love myself well, I am not very capable of loving my neighbor well either. I am not talking about being selfish but loving and taking care of the temple God has given me. My neighbors are those people God puts in my life (wife, children, actual neighbors, coworkers, friends, family). And I am not able to love others well if I don't love myself well. I can't take care of those God has put in my life if I don't put on my oxygen mask first. However in this process we do need to be cautious that our self-care doesn't turn into selfishness. If our self-care time is causing us to neglect our families and responsibilities, then we need to reevaluate.

After this revelation from God my life did not suddenly become easier. I didn't all of a sudden win the lottery and no longer need to work. In fact I was still in the same position working all the time and not getting enough sleep, but I knew things needed to change. I met with Jaime and talked to her about what God was saying to me and discussed what changes that needed to happen. I needed to make changes in my relationship with food and increase my exercise. I spoke with health professionals about my diet and lifestyle. I also examined my schedule and realized that the only time I had in my day was to get up early to exercise. Now mind you I am not a morning person, but that was the only choice I had at that time. I prayed for God to make the sleep I was getting to be more restful for me and help me to make the transition to getting up early. I set the alarm and got started.

In Psalm 63:1 (New King James Version) David writes "O God, You are my God; Early will I seek you..." I kept those words in my mind as I tried to peel my eyes open, and God began to open a plan for me to follow. I have come to realize years later that these disciplines in my life would not have occurred if I didn't do them first thing in my day. Years later I still follow this same plan each morning:

1. Gratitude- The first thing I do when I wake up is to say a prayer of thanks to God (1 Thessalonians 5:18). I say "Thank you Lord for a new day and the breath in my lungs, the bed I slept in, the roof over my head, and for my wife and family. Thank you that my eyes opened, that my heart beats and my hands and feet are working."
2. Service- The second thing I do is make coffee, which at first seemed like more of a habit than anything else. However when I thought about it I make coffee every morning for myself and bring a cup to my wife, so the second thing I do is love and serve my wife. I have done this for 20 years now and it wasn't until writing this that I understood the importance of it. A true leader serves others, and I am beginning my day with that practice.
3. Knowledge- Once the caffeine kicks in and my mind is somewhat focused and working I read God's Word. I open my playbook. I ask the Holy Spirit to teach me what He needs me to learn that day (1 Corinthians 2:11-14) and read a chapter of the Bible. It gives me something to think about and chew on for the day.
4. Connection- I'm in my mid 40s so stretching is essential if I want to be able to run, climb, or move effectively. So every morning I take about 10 to 15 minutes to stretch and breathe.

I connect with how my body is doing and feeling. Some days I spend more time than that, and sometimes I need to do this multiple times a day.

5. <u>Movement</u>- I then exercise for 30 to 45 minutes. I spend time running, hiking, doing yoga, doing push-ups or pull-ups or free weights or something. I try if at all possible to do this outside every day. It gives me a chance to pray out loud and gets me connected to nature. We are designed to move and our bodies get stiff and tired when we stop. As I like to say to myself "If I don't use it, I'll lose it."

This game plan took some time for me to put into practice every day, but once I committed to it I have seen the results in my health (physically and spiritually) to this day. I try to do this seven days a week in some fashion. I'm not perfect, but it is what I shoot for.

Also in this plan there were some important things God impressed upon me *not* to do. Before this time I would start my day looking at work emails and social media accounts and other things on the internet. God was pretty clear to me that He didn't want me starting my day off filling my mind with that stuff. I would get to all that later on in the day, but He wanted me to focus on Him first.

Another game plan God spoke to me about was my prayer life. I have a commute to my job like most people. It takes me approximately 30 minutes to get to work. I used to listen to music or podcasts, but during one of my times of fasting God spoke to me about using that time to pray, and He gave me some specifics on how to do that. This is what the prayer schedule looks like:

<u>Monday</u>- My mind, body and spirit (I go from my head to my feet):
1. Mind- I pray over my thoughts (Philippians 4:8) and for wisdom (James 1:5) first.
2. Eyes- I pray over my eyes that I am careful what I look at (Job 31:1) and to guard me from falling into lust.
3. Mouth- that my words may "encourage one another daily (Hebrews 3:13 New International Version)" and to "speak the truth in love (Ephesians 4:15 New Living Translation)"
4. Ears- that I may be "quick to listen, slow to speak and slow to become angry (James 1:19 New International Version)"
5. Shoulders- that I may carry my own load that God has allotted for me (Galatians 6:5) and that I may take His yoke upon me and find rest (Matthew 11:29-30)
6. Hands- that whatever I put them to they may prosper (Deuteronomy 30:9)

7. Heart- I pray over my physical heart and my spiritual heart for God to "Create in me a clean heart (Psalm 51:10 English Standard Version)."
8. Vital organs- I pray over my lungs and liver and kidneys and stomach and so on, and I bind cancer in Jesus name (Matthew 18:18).
9. Back, Hips, IT Bands, Hamstrings, Quadriceps, Knees, Calves, and Feet- I pray healing over these parts (Isaiah 53:5), so I can keep myself moving and healthy.

Tuesday- Our pastors, churches and other ministries we support or are involved in

Wednesday- My family: nuclear and extended

Thursday- Friends, neighbors, community and their salvations ("…that the goodness of God leads you to repentance" Romans 2:4 New King James Version)

Friday- The persecuted church (Hebrews 13:3) (there are organizations like Voice of the Martyrs that provide great resources and prayer materials to help you to pray in this area) and also local, state and federal governments (1 Timothy 2:1-4)

Some years God leads me in some pretty specific ways and other times He gives me areas to focus on and grow in. For example in 2019 He impressed upon me these words: Leadership, Gratitude and Generosity. 2019 turned out to be a pretty tough year for my wife and me personally and professionally. There were a lot of changes and heartaches. In 2020 the Holy Spirit gave me these words through my fasting time: Obedience, Trust and Focus. Little did I know how much I would need those things through that crazy year and the pandemic that followed.

These are some examples of game plans God has given me. Things will most likely be different for you as you diligently seek Him. Your game plan will look different. When you were an athlete your coach had to tailor a plan for you according to your fitness, skill and position. What I have found over the years, which was true when I was competing, is that I only get the results when I am consistent (day in, day out, year in, year out) with executing those plans.

In closing, the impetus for writing this chapter came out of a coaching season where I had a team who won their league during the fall season, only losing one game. They didn't make as far of a postseason run as they wanted, but they had a very good season by any measure.

Many of the members of that team along with a few others from another team rejoined in the spring of that next year to play in a select league. There was a lot of excitement at the beginning of the spring season as the guys got back together and were hoping to pick up where they left off from their success in the fall. Long story short during that spring season we did not win one single game. Yep, not one game. It was tough on them and tough on me as a coach.

Admittedly the competition in the spring season was better, but the practices, the fitness and the expectations were the same from the fall. The difference was the team was committed in the fall, and in the spring they were not. A number of players didn't show up for practices on a continual basis, and some didn't even come to games. It was frustrating for the players who showed up for every practice and game and caused a lot of dissension. Eventually we got through the season, and at my end of the season talk with the team I used these words to summarize how things went: Potential Without Commitment. I explained that it didn't matter how much skill each guy on the team had. If they weren't committed to giving it everything they had, they would always fall short of how good they could potentially be. The same rings true for us in life and in our walk with God today. In order for us to live the life God has for us, we need to put in the work. I have plenty of people in my life who ask me to pray for them which I gladly do, but are they also praying and seeking God themselves? To me it's like asking someone else to get healthy and in shape for you by saying "Can you eat right and exercise for me, so that I can be healthy?" We all know it doesn't quite work that way.

Chapter 9

How to Handle the Losing Seasons

"I've missed more than 9,000 shots in my career. I've lost almost 300 games. 26 times, I've been trusted to take the game winning shot and missed. I've failed over and over and over again in my life. And that is why I succeed."

-Michael Jordan

       The reality is we are going to have losing seasons. Some of these seasons are due to our choices, and some of them are just the trials of life. Jesus warned his team, his disciples, of this when He told them in John 16:33 (New King James Version), "These things I have spoken to you, that in Me you may have peace. In the world you will have tribulation; but be of good cheer, I have overcome the world." His disciples left everything they had to follow Him to spread the good news of the gospel, and Jesus tells them that they will have tribulation. It's a guarantee. Anybody who tells you if you just do this or that or plug in the right choices or formula that your life will be carefree is just selling you something. Don't buy it. God spoke to me as I was finishing up coaching a soccer season in the fall of 2019 and said it was a time to take a break from coaching and focus on writing this book. I had no idea at the time what the world would like the following year as we all battled through the Coronavirus pandemic of 2020. Like many of you my wife and I were trying to hold down jobs, and she was also trying to be a teacher for all three of our kids who were doing virtual distance learning. My children had no school, no sports, no church and limited social contact. We were fortunate to remain working, but many people were not. None of this trial or tribulation was due to some poor parenting decision or some other unwise choice any of us made, but we all had to struggle through it.

       Solomon also wrote about this in Ecclesiastes 3:1-8 (New King James Version):

> To everything there is a season,
> A time for every purpose under heaven:
>
> A time to be born,
> And a time to die;
> A time to plant,
> And a time to pluck what is planted;

A time to kill,
And a time to heal;
A time to break down,
And a time to build up;
A time to weep,
And a time to laugh;
A time to mourn,
And a time to dance;
A time to cast away stones,
And a time to gather stones;
A time to embrace,
And a time to refrain from embracing;
A time to gain,
And a time to lose;
A time to keep,
And a time to throw away;
A time to tear,
And a time to sew;
A time to keep silence,
And a time to speak;
A time to love,
And a time to hate;
A time of war,
And a time of peace.

In verse 6 it says "a time to gain, and a time to lose." In life, as in athletics, we will lose. We can put in all the work, commitment and discipline, and there will be times we still lose. I don't say this to be a downer or pessimistic but just to state the truth. I quoted Michael Jordan, which most people argue is the greatest basketball player of all time, at the beginning of the chapter. He said "I've failed over and over and over again in my life. And that is why I succeed."

So what are the losing seasons supposed to teach us about success?

Looking at the football career of Peyton Manning gives us an example of these different "seasons." Manning had a record of 34-5 and threw for more than 7,000 yards as a high school quarterback. He was highly recruited coming out of high school and chose to play college football at the University of Tennessee. Over his four years playing there he threw for 11,201 yards and set 42 conference, school and NCAA records. He was then drafted as the first overall pick by the Indianapolis Colts in 1998. Manning obviously had a pretty long run of a winning season.

During his rookie year with the Colts however the team went 3-13, and Manning still holds the NFL record for most interceptions thrown by a rookie with 28. From that point it would take him nine years to win his first Super Bowl in 2007. The Colts would make it to the Super Bowl again in 2009, but this time they would lose to the Saints. Manning went from nine years of struggling in the beginning of his NFL career to the pinnacle of competing and winning until 2011. On September 8, 2011 he underwent the third of three neck surgeries he had in the previous 19 months, and he missed the entire 2011 season. The Colts then took Andrew Luck as their new quarterback in the 2012 draft and released Manning, the guy who took their struggling team in 1998 to two Super Bowl appearances and the only Super Bowl win in Indianapolis Colts franchise history.

He then signed a contract with the Denver Broncos in March of 2012. He made his comeback from neck surgery to win his fifth MVP in 2013 and set NFL records for the most touchdowns (55) and passing yards (5,477) in a single season. He made two more Super Bowl appearances, losing in 2014 and winning in 2016, after which he retired (Peyton Manning Biography, 2020). As you can see from Manning's story there was "a time to gain, and a time to lose (Ecclesiastes 3:6 New King James Version)."

It goes without saying that no one likes a losing season. In fact no one likes to lose a game. If we're honest no one even likes to lose in a scrimmage at the end of practice either. Even in our *everyone gets a ribbon or trophy at the end of the season* society nowadays in which our young children are not supposed to keep score when they play games against one another, everyone still keeps track of the score and who won. Teams like to win. As a coach everyone likes you when your team wins. Players have more fun when they win. But the reality is we can't win all the time. Nobody wants to hear that, but it's true.

It is during the losing seasons however where we grow and improve. I will be the first to admit I don't want to hear that. We all want life to be easy with no problems, but it's not. When things are easy we don't think about how we can improve or change. We don't analyze what is not going right. Why would we? We're winning.

There are two concepts that we learned as athletes that can help us endure, learn and even succeed during the losing seasons of life: playing through the pain and playing until the last whistle.

1. Playing Through the Pain

All of us as athletes had those times where we played through the pain. We taped up that injury and got back out there. We might not have been as effective as we were before, but we weren't going to sit it out. Our team needed us. Speaking of Michael Jordan, some of you might remember in Game 5 of the 1997 NBA Finals against the Utah Jazz when he played with the flu and food poisoning. The series was tied 2-2, and he helped his team secure that pivotal victory which led to the Bulls winning the NBA championship that year.

Stories and experiences like that are what we would refer to as a gut check. It is there to push us to rise above the circumstances we face, and see what we are made of. Paul writes about how this feels in 2 Corinthians 4:8-9 (New International Version) when he says "We are hard pressed on every side, but not crushed; perplexed, but not in despair; persecuted, but not abandoned; struck down, but not destroyed."

Injuries come hand in hand with athletics. There are setbacks. You are moving along, performing well, winning games, and then one second later it all changes. You sprain something, tear something or break something. It stops you in your tracks and takes you out of the game. Some injuries are short-term and some stick with you for quite a while.

In my 8th grade year playing middle school football we had a game against our middle school rivalry. Our school and theirs fed the high school I attended, so it was big bragging rights to win that game. We may have been tied or were losing towards the end of the game. I can't remember exactly, but we needed to score. We had the ball and were driving down the field. I was playing quarterback, and the coach called an option play going to the right side of the field. The ball was snapped, and I started running to the right side. I faked the pitch to the running back and kept the ball. I was hit out of bounds after gaining some yards. After the tackle I was down on my back, and a player from the other team who was chasing me down jumped in the air and put his cleats into my stomach knocking the wind out of me. The referee didn't see it. I slowly got up, and the opposing player stood there looking down on me putting his helmet against mine. I was pretty dazed, and he spouted off some cuss words and something to the effect of "Next time stay down!"

My eyes focused on his for a second, and I stepped away angry. I was thinking to myself he should have taken me out of this game. He should have injured me, because now we're going to win this game. I drove the offense down the rest of the field, and we scored a touchdown. Our defense stopped them on the next possession. We got the ball back and began to burn the clock on the remaining minutes of the last quarter.

I remember it got down to a third down and short yardage situation. If we got the first down, we could snap the ball, take a knee a few times and time would expire. I got the play from the coach, and told the guys in the huddle that I was going to do a hard count and try to draw their defense offsides. It worked like a charm, and we got a new set of downs, ran out the clock and won the game.

I sometimes think back on that game and smile. At this point in my life though it reminds me of what the devil is trying to do to most of us. First off he doesn't play fair. He'll come in with the late hit when you're lying on your back and kick you while you're down. He comes to steal and kill and destroy (John 10:10). The devil also goes after us through our spouse or our kids. He goes after our finances and our health. We need to always remember when the injuries come that "You are of God, little children, and have overcome them, because He who is in you is greater than he who is in the world (1 John 4:4 New King James Version)." We are on God's team. We are on the winning side. We need to catch our breath, stand back up, focus our eyes, square our jaw and remind ourselves "The Lord is on my side; I will not fear. What can man do to me (Psalm 118:6 English Standard Version)?"

After that we need to take action. We need to march the ball down the field and score. We need to remind the devil of his place. He might knock us out of the game for a play or two, but we are going to have the victory. We may have a season where our marriages are struggling or our kids are headed in the wrong direction or we got bad news health wise or we lose our job, and the devil is yelling in our face "Next time stay down!" Remember he is a defeated foe, and we just need to get back up. He knows as long as we stay in the game, he will lose.

Sometimes playing through the pain is for a play or two. We can dust ourselves off and get back out there, however sometimes we have injuries that sideline us for a long time. I mentioned in Chapter 2 about my high school soccer career and how I was playing on the varsity team as a sophomore until I sustained a bad ankle injury. That injury stayed with me throughout the rest of my high school years. I couldn't seem to get to a place where I was not consistently reinjuring it. It also went from a physical injury to a mental one. I began to lose my confidence in myself and so did my coaches. In my junior year I started playing on the JV team instead and wasn't a starter for one game my entire senior year. It was my dream to get a scholarship to play college soccer. I had played the game since I was four years old. I had competed at the highest club levels and played internationally for a summer as well. I had worked endless hours on my game, and this *losing season* in my career threatened to steal my dream. I got some advice at one point in my senior year on some exercises I needed to do in order to prevent my ankle injuries. They were painful, but I went after it and never had issues with my ankles again.

Joseph's Story

A story in the Bible that reminds me of someone who had to endure playing through the pain for a long time is Joseph. His story is found in Genesis chapters 37-50. He was the second youngest boy in the family. Joseph had 11 brothers, but he was his dad's favorite. His dad Israel gave him an expensive decorative robe to display to all of the boys that he was the favored one. This obviously caused some dissension in the ranks, and his brothers didn't like him very much to say the least. To make matters worse Joseph had a couple of dreams in which the symbolism in the dreams were that all of his brothers would bow down to him. He was 17 years old at the time, so I guess we should forgive his impulsivity of expressing those dreams to all of his brothers who already despised him, but the brothers weren't going to let it slide.

The story goes on, and his brothers are now out working while Joseph is at home hanging out with his dad (another knock against him). Dad sends him out to go check on his brothers to see how things are going out in the fields. Israel doesn't send Joseph out there to give his brothers a hand. He sends him out to check on them and report back. The brothers see him in the distance flaunting his colorful robe and coming their way. They decide to kill him and tell their father he was killed by a wild animal. One of the brothers, Reuben, thinks that's a bit harsh and convinces the other brothers to just throw him in a well and leave him there. Reuben's plan was to come back later and rescue Joseph.

Afterwards they sit down to eat some lunch and see a caravan coming, and they decide to sell Joseph to them as a slave. Reuben might have been off relieving himself (the Bible doesn't say that, but I'm taking a guess at what happened), and the brothers pull Joseph out and sell him off. Reuben gets back from doing his business and sees that Joseph is gone. He confronts his brothers who tell him what happened. They then decide to kill a goat and spread the blood on Joseph's robe and tell their dad an animal killed his son.

The caravan heads down to Egypt and sells him to Potiphar, the captain of the guard for Pharaoh. God was with Joseph and gave him success in Potiphar's house, so much so that he was put in charge of his entire estate. Joseph was also quite a handsome guy, and Potiphar's wife takes notice of him and wants to sleep with him. Joseph turns her down. Now keep in mind that he was a 17 year old guy at the time he was sold to Potiphar, with his hormones at their peak, so this was not an easy task. She doesn't take rejection well and propositions him again. Joseph remains steadfast and flees temptation, but she grabs his cloak as he runs out of the house. He is now naked outside the house, and she then accuses him of raping her. Keeping in mind that Joseph is still a slave, there is no trial. Potiphar just throws him in prison. His word means nothing in this case. He is faithful to God, does what is right and is still imprisoned. However in spite of being in prison, God is still with him (Genesis 39:21), and Joseph begins to gain favor with the prison warden.

This is extremely important to remember when we go through those losing seasons. God hasn't forgotten us. God still has a plan even when we don't understand it. I don't know why Joseph ended up in prison, but God does. God was preparing him for the next steps in his life. As hard as it can be at times, there are things the Coach needs us to learn during those losing seasons.

Joseph does interpret some dreams for a couple of guys that were in prison with him. One of those guys gets a favorable report and gets out, and the other guy gets impaled. Joseph asks the guy who gets out to remember him and put in a good word for him, so he can get out as well. The guy does remember Joseph, however it was two years after his request when Pharaoh ends up having a dream that no one in his kingdom can interpret. Pharaoh gets Joseph out of prison and tells him the dreams he has been having. With God's power Joseph is able to interpret the dream, and in one day Pharaoh pulls him out of prison and puts him in charge of his entire palace.

That is another important thing to remember. We don't know how long our losing seasons last, but God can turn things around very quickly.

Joseph is now in charge of the world's superpower at the time and has the task of getting it prepared for an upcoming seven year famine. He is now 30 years old (Genesis 41:46). That's 13 years since he was sold into slavery, which is a bit longer than a couple of bad days in a row. He develops a system to store up food during the abundant years, so there will be provisions for the seven years of famine that are coming. The famine hits, and the world begins to starve. The word on the street though is that there is food down in Egypt, so the same brothers who wanted to kill him and sold him into slavery make the trek to Egypt to buy some food. However one of the brothers stays behind with dad.

When they get there Joseph recognizes them, but they don't recognize him. He questions his brothers harshly, and they reveal that they left one of the brothers back in Canaan. The next few chapters are a bit of a wild goose chase in which Joseph sends them back to get the brother in Canaan but keeps one of the other brothers with him in Egypt. He also pranks them a couple of times before he finally reveals to them who he is. The brothers are scared out of their minds when they find out who he is, however Joseph's perspective from persevering through the losing seasons of his life is not one of revenge or spite as is shown in this section of scripture:

> Then Joseph said to his brothers, "Come close to me." When they had done so, he said "I am your brother Joseph, the one you sold into Egypt!" And now, do not be distressed and do not be angry with yourselves for selling me here, because it was to save lives that God sent me ahead of you. For two years there has been famine in the land, and for the next five years there will be no plowing and reaping. But God sent me ahead of you to preserve for you a remnant on earth and to save your lives by a great deliverance.
>
> "So then, it was not you who sent me here, but God. He made me father to Pharaoh, lord of his entire household and ruler of all Egypt. Now hurry back to my father and say to him, 'This is what your son Joseph says: God has made me lord of all Egypt. Come down to me; don't delay
> (Genesis 45:4-9 New International Version).'"

At this point Pharaoh catches wind of the news that Joseph's brothers are in town, and he tells them that they are welcome to stay and gives them land for them and their animals. They then depart Egypt and go back to Canaan to get their father. The family reunites and are able to survive the famine.

As you read through Joseph's story you can see the ups and downs, the winning seasons and the losing seasons. You can see a man who played through the pain and in turn saved the entire nation of Israel from perishing. You see a man filled with character and hope that came from suffering and perseverance (Romans 5:3-4).

2. Playing Until the Last Whistle

One of the tougher things to accomplish as a coach is to keep your team's head in the game when they're losing, to try and convince them mentally to keep pushing to come back and win. Some players keep going no matter what, but with a lot of players you can see the air go out of their balloon so to speak. That happens to most us if we were being honest when things are going south with your marriage, your kids, your job and your health, and it all seems to hit at the same time. It is the proverbial "When it rains it pours" situation in life. I have noticed in my time as a therapist that some men have a distinct reaction to these scenarios, myself included at times, in which they want to just throw in the towel. They want to quit their job, leave their wife, walk out on their kids, etc. The sad thing is that many men do.

We have to remember that it isn't over till God says it's over. All of these pressures and negative things can be stacked against you, but if you stay in the fight you can still win. If you give up, then you've already lost. In Galatians 6:9 (New International Version) it says "Let us not become weary in doing good, for at the proper time we will reap a harvest if we do not give up." The flip side of that verse is that if we *do* give up, we won't reap the harvest.

Another play from the book to remember in this regard is Philippians 4:13 (New Living Translation) where it says "For I can do everything through Christ, who gives me strength." Note where the strength comes from. It does not come from us. It comes from Jesus. Knowing that will give us the mindset we need to play until the last whistle. It isn't all on me. God's grace and strength will get me through, but I have to choose to keep fighting.

The Curse of the Bambino

A great depiction of that mindset comes from the 30 for 30 ESPN documentary *Four Days in October*. The documentary follows the 2004 American League Championship Series between the New York Yankees and the Boston Red Sox. The Red Sox had not won a World Series since 1918, a winning drought known as the Curse of the Bambino, after the Red Sox sold Babe Ruth ("The Bambino") to the New York Yankees after the 1919 season. That's a pretty long losing season when you think about it. To make matters worse, the Red Sox lost the first three games of the series in 2004, and no team in baseball history had ever come back from a 3-0 deficit in the playoffs. The Red Sox needed to win the next four games to advance to the World Series finals. You would think with those kind of odds stacked against you, you would hang your head low and hope things ended soon, but not so with outfielder Kevin Millar.

In the documentary the camera follows him as he talks to a reporter on the sideline and to his teammates on the field before the game. Two statements stuck out to me from that montage when he says:

1. "To me it was give me that wire. Let's talk about what needs to happen. We have a game to win tonight. Don't let us win this game tonight. Then they get Petey, then they get Schill game 6 and game 7 anything happens."

2. "Don't count the Sox out. You cannot count the Sox out. If there's a group of idiots that can do it, it's us. It hasn't happened in the history of baseball, but don't let us win today (Check, 2010, 5:29)."

You can hear the *never say die attitude* in his statements. The team is backed into a corner and facing something that has never been done before. Millar never loses hope. All he needs is one win, and it all could change.

That is the same for all of us as we face the losing seasons of life. We might be knocked down, but we're not out. Job lost everything he had as we talked about in the first chapter, but he didn't quit. He hung in there. The devil may have injured you. Life may have backed you into the corner and presented you with impossible odds, but all you need is one win. The Red Sox do go on to win the series, winning the next four games. They then sweep the St. Louis Cardinals to become the 2004 World Series Champions.

There are many other comeback stories out there in sports and in life. You might have one from your own sports career that puts a smile on your face when you think about it. The reason it makes you smile is that you didn't lose hope. Even though you were down, you persevered and won. Remembering that and keeping that benchmark in your mind is so important when we face things in life where we just want to quit.

You might be down by 10 points with two minutes to go in the fourth quarter in your marriage, and the opposing team has the ball. What do you do?

You may be in a best of seven series and down three games in your relationship with your kids. What do you do?

You may have been handed the baton for the last leg of the relay, and your team is in last place when it comes to your finances. What do you do?

Do you count yourself out or fight with everything you've got left?

We discussed in Chapter 2 how our focus or our mindset determines our actions. We need to first have the mentality that we will keep going and keep pushing no matter what difficulties or what odds we face. We are not alone in this, and there is a purpose to why we are going through this season of life.

Trust the Process

In 2015 the Philadelphia 76ers used a phrase "Trust the Process" referring to its team rebuilding process. They had T-shirts, bracelets, stickers and fans chanting the phrase. As I write this in 2020 it's a bit uncertain how well that process is going as they were swept by the Boston Celtics in the first round of the NBA playoffs, but one never knows. In any case the phrase is one we need to keep in the forefront of our minds as we endure through our losing seasons.

Do we trust God and the process He is taking us through?

I've heard it said that if God showed us the entirety of our lives at one time we probably wouldn't want to walk it out. That may be true and could be the reason God tells us to not worry about tomorrow and just focus on today (Matthew 6:34). We talked about Joseph earlier, and he is one of those few people in which God showed him the end result first, not just the step ahead of him. However even with being shown the end result, he had to go through his process. Joseph may have been shown that he would rule over his brothers and his family, but he had to endure his process to be ready for that role. God needed to take him through a 13 year losing season to get him to the place where he could effectively do what God had for him to do. It is no different with us.

In James 1:2-4 (New International Version) it says "Consider it pure joy, my brothers and sisters, whenever you face trials of many kinds, because you know that the testing of your faith produces perseverance. Let perseverance finish its work so that you may be mature and complete, not lacking anything." God's goal and our goal for ourselves should be to become "mature and complete, not lacking anything." The issue with fulfilling that goal is that we need to "let perseverance finish its work" in us. We are in charge. We can stay on that train and trust God or get off at the next station.

The difficult part is that the way perseverance is produced is by "the testing of your faith," and that testing comes "whenever you face trials of many kinds." This process shouldn't come as a surprise for us who were athletes, because to get to a place where our game was "complete, not lacking anything" we needed to go through trial after trial. None of us stepped on the field at game time and expected we wouldn't take a few hits. We knew we would. It's the same in life. If you're in the game, you're going to take some hits.

Joseph's losing season lasted 13 years. It took Peyton Manning nine years to get back to the top and win his first Super Bowl. It took the Boston Red Sox 86 years to win another championship! It goes without saying that any of our losing seasons will feel too long. No one likes to feel uncomfortable, and no one likes to lose. However it is vital for us to understand that these are the seasons of our lives that God uses to sharpen us and get us ready for the next level. These are the times when we examine ourselves to see where we need to get better. As athletes we needed to put in the extra time on the practice field, in the weight room, with our coaches, studying game film and going through play after play with our teammates in order to improve and learn from those seasons.

In Jeremiah 17:7-8 (New King James Version) it says:

Blessed is the man who trusts in the Lord,
And whose hope is in the Lord.
For he shall be like a tree planted by the waters,
Which spreads out its roots by the river,
And will not fear when heat comes;
But its leaf will be green,
And will not be anxious in the year of drought,
Nor will cease from yielding fruit.

"Blessed is the man who trusts in the Lord" during the losing season. The man who trusts the process. He is not hopeless. His "hope is in the Lord," and the lessons God is taking him through. He will not be moved in spite of his present circumstances. He is "a tree planted by the waters." The roots of his spirit are deep and connected to the river, to the source of his strength. Heat will come. Drought will come, but he will not fear. He will continue to produce fruit in his life.

Joseph still had success and favor even while he was in prison, because he stayed planted and rooted in the things of God. He was unable to do this in his own strength. In Isaiah 40:31 (New Living Translation) it says "But those who trust in the Lord will find new strength."

We need that "new strength" during those losing seasons. We need to spend time rooted to God to get that strength. Just as we would with our coach after a losing season, we need to ask God what we need to do and where we need to improve. Spend time in prayer listening to that "still small voice" and write down what you hear. Spend time with your pastor or mentors or your team of friends asking for feedback and prayer. Meet with a financial advisor and develop a budget and stick to it. Stop buying things you can't afford. Meet with your doctor and a trainer and take on your health. Get rid of those unhealthy food and drinks in your home. Meet with a therapist. Cut out the distractions and toxic relationships. Put the phone away when you get home from work. Date your spouse. Pursue them. Get off those websites that pollute your mind and heart. Examine your attitude and how you treat God and others. Get back to church. Love your neighbor. Volunteer in your community. Learn what you need to learn and apply it. The reality is just like your coach back in the day wanted you to learn and get better from your losing season, so does God. He wants us to learn and get better for the next season and level in our lives. So let's "not be anxious in the year of drought." Don't throw in the towel or count yourself out. The Coach is with us, developing a strategy for our game to get better. Trust the process and walk it out, so we don't have to relearn those lessons from our losing seasons but come out with "new strength."

Chapter 10

<u>How to Be Your Family's Team Captain</u>

"It is easier to build strong children than to repair broken men."

-Frederick Douglas

This chapter is going to look at our role as husbands and fathers and some principles from God's Word regarding those roles. When I was thinking and praying through this section God gave me this thought to ponder in terms of our children and how He uses them to shape and grow us:

We are given the team we need, not the team we want.

Also our relationships with our wives can exist along a continuum of being the most rewarding on one hand as well as the most frustrating on the other. I'm pretty confident my wife would say that same thing about me too. God uses these relationships to grow us and sharpen us to be more like Him, to better understand His heart for us, His children. I have honestly grown and have been stretched more in so many ways personally and spiritually in my role as a husband and father than in any other role I've had.

In my third year on my college track team I was chosen to be the team captain for the sprinters. Looking back I'm not sure I took the responsibility all that seriously, but it was still an honor to be chosen by my coaches and teammates for the position.

What if we viewed our roles as husbands and fathers through the lens of being our family's team captain? What would our leadership and ownership of our families look like? Would we look upon our position as husband and father with that same sense of honor?

Qualities of a Team Captain

      In an article written by Daniel Benjamin he discusses the importance of team captains in the game of basketball. His view on the importance of player leadership is that even if your coach is a great leader, players tend to respond better to peer motivation and peer pressure. This model also fits for our roles as leaders in our homes. As discussed in Chapter 4 God is an incredible coach, but He needs us as men to live out His game plan in order to lead our families. God needs us to model His love for our families.

The article goes on to list 10 qualities of an effective team captain:

1. You must be self-motivated. Team captains are the heart and soul of a team, going all out every minute you are on the floor during games as well as in practice. You should be the first one at practice and one of the last to leave.
2. Team captains firmly believe that the best interest of the team always comes first.
3. Team captains are bold, tenacious, fearless, prepared, fluid and enthusiastic.
4. Team leaders are great listeners and have a thirst to improve. When a coach tells you something, you should listen to the meaning of the words and not how it is said. If a coach didn't care, he wouldn't bother to help you become the best player possible.
5. Team captains expect and demand the best from themselves and their teammates.
6. Know your role. A key part of being a leader is knowing your role on the team (scorer, rebounder, shutdown defender, sixth man, etc.). If you don't know, ask.
7. Team captains choose their words carefully. The words of the team captain mean more than that of any other player.
8. Encourages teammates. A good leader keeps the team upbeat and positive. If a teammate is down, the captain picks the player's spirits up.
9. Understand that mistakes will be made. Team leaders can't get down on themselves or others when mistakes happen, because if you do others will follow. So instead of chastising yourself or a teammate, learn from the mistake and move on. Simple statements like "I got you next time" or "Relax, I will get the ball again next time" will do wonders for a player's confidence after a mistake.

10. Team captains do not allow others to talk negatively about the team. You should take any insult about a team member as an insult against the whole team (Benjamin, n.d.).

What a challenging list! Now let's look at each quality and what God has to say about each one from His word:

1. Love the Lord your God with all your heart and with all your soul and with all your strength (Deuteronomy 6:5 New International Version).

   We lead by example with our actions, not just by what we say. If we want our *team* to play as hard as they can, we must give our all and do so first.

2. Don't be selfish; don't try to impress others. Be humble, thinking of others as better than yourselves (Philippians 2:3 New Living Translation).

   God wants us to put our families' interests before our own.

3. For God has not given us a spirit of fear, but of power and of love and of a sound mind (2 Timothy 1:7 New King James Version).

   We need to lead our team with confidence, strength and consistency.

4. Come and listen to my counsel. I'll share my heart with you and make you wise (Proverbs 1:23 New Living Translation).

   As team captains it is vital we spend time with God in order to get the proper direction to lead our teams.

5. Whatever you do, work at it with you whole being, for the Lord and not for men (Colossians 3:23 Berean Study Bible).

   We cannot expect our families to work hard and do their best if we don't ourselves.

6. For just as each of us has one body with many members, and these members do not all have the same function, so in Christ

we, though many, form one body, and each member belongs to all the others. We have different gifts, according to the grace given to each of us (Romans 12:4-6a New International Version).

Play your position and do it as well as you can. You are not gifted in everything. Trust your team. Other members of your family are better than you in different areas.

7. Fathers, do not provoke your children to anger by the way you treat them. Rather, bring them up with the discipline and instruction that comes from the Lord (Ephesians 6:4 New Living Translation).

   "The words of the team captain mean more than that of any other player." We need to be careful of our words as fathers. They carry a lot of weight.

8. For you know that we dealt with each of you as a father deals with his own children, encouraging, comforting and urging you to live lives worthy of God, who calls you into his kingdom and glory (1 Thessalonians 2:11-12 New International Version).

   Your leadership, words and attitude set the tone and atmosphere in your home. God wants that to be one of encouragement and hope.

9. Be kind to one another, tenderhearted, forgiving one another, as God in Christ forgave you (Ephesians 4:32 English Standard Version).

   You are not perfect, and neither is anyone on your team. Forgive quickly and learn from it.

10. Get rid of all bitterness, rage, anger, harsh words, and slander, along with every form of malice (Ephesians 4:31 New Living Translation).

   We are to treat our family members with respect and expect the same from them.

Leading Through Service

As Christians we are called to follow the teaching and example of Jesus. Jesus never married and didn't have any children, so we can't look specifically to that time in His life. However He did lead a team. He had 12 disciples on His team as well as many others who followed Him.

So how did He lead? What was His leadership style so to speak? How did He captain His team?

In Matthew 20 the disciples are arguing with each other about who among them will be the greatest in heaven. Jesus gathers the team around him and says "You know that the rulers of the Gentiles lord it over them, and those who are great exercise authority over them. Yet it shall not be so among you; but whoever desires to become great among you, let him be your servant. And whoever desires to be first among you, let him be your slave- just as the Son of Man did not come to be served, but to serve, and to give His life a ransom for many (Matthew 20:25-28 New King James Version)."

Jesus didn't come to be served but to serve. He addresses his disciples' desire for greatness by saying "whoever desires to become great among you, let him be your servant." Jesus preached that power and authority comes from serving others. This is where we have to start as men in order to be the team captain for our families that God needs us to be. We need to have a heart of service towards our wife and kids. It is not an attitude of what you can do for me, but it is an attitude of how can I take care of you. Jesus lived out this attitude with his team of disciples which is vividly depicted in the act of Him washing his disciples' feet. Their feet in those days would have been covered in dirt and animal feces. This would not have been a pleasant task by any means. He even washed the feet of Judas when He knew he would betray Him.

As Jesus finishes up it says in John 13:12-17 (New King James Version), "So when He had washed their feet, taken His garments, and sat down again, He said to them, 'Do you know what I have done to you? You call Me Teacher and Lord, and you say well, for so I am. If I then, your Lord and Teacher, have washed your feet, you also ought to wash one another's feet. For I have given you an example, that you should do as I have done to you. Most assuredly, I say to you, a servant is not greater than his master; nor is he who is sent greater than he who sent him. If you know these things, blessed are you if you do them.'"

Do we want to be blessed? Of course we all want to be blessed in our lives and in our marriages and families. Jesus lays out a path to blessing for His team. His path is for us to lead others through serving them.

Do you want to be a great leader? Be a great servant.

Do you want your children to be leaders and make an impact in the world? Teach them to serve.

Our primary goal in leading our families should not be their happiness, despite what the culture says. We all want ourselves, our wives and children to be happy, but happiness is a fleeting emotion. God calls us to be holy (1 Peter 1:16) and to help others (Acts 20:35), and those should be our primary goals as we captain our teams.

Love and Honor Your Vice-Captain

On a soccer team there is a captain and a vice-captain. A vice-captain is a person who fills in when the captain is not able to play or lead the team. A somewhat famous example of this scenario (if you're a soccer fan) is the 2012 Champions League Final between Chelsea and Bayern Munich. Chelsea's captain John Terry was suspended for the match after getting a red card in the preceding game. Frank Lampard, who was the vice-captain for the team, stepped into that leadership role for the final game and led his team to victory winning 4-3 in a penalty shoot-out.

I like the view of this relationship of captain and vice-captain as it relates to marriage. Often times the marriage relationship in Christian circles gets likened to a thought process of superiority and inferiority. Way too often in Christian circles and in Christian marriages (at least in some of the marriage therapy sessions I've done through the years) men are quick to assert this pecking order and reference Ephesians 5:22-24 (New International Version) where it says:

> Wives, submit yourselves to your own husbands as you do to the Lord. For the husband is the head of the wife as Christ is the head of the church, his body, of which he is the Savior. Now as the church submits to Christ, so also wives should submit to their husbands in everything.

From these verses I will listen to the husbands tell me something to the effect of "You see. God's word says she needs to do what I tell her to." I hear them out and then reference them to the preceding verse of Ephesians 5:21 where it says "Submit to one another out of reverence for Christ." Again I'm no theologian, but it would seem that there are times when I am to submit to my wife as well. I then proceed to ask "If you want your wife to submit to you, are you living a life that is worthy of submission?" Most times they are not, and that is why they are in my office.

I want it to be well understood that I am not trying to argue against God's design of men being the head of house. I am however wanting to offer a different perspective as it relates to the example of the captain and vice-captain relationship. For this example I'd like us to view the marriage relationship through the lens of the husband being the captain and the wife being the vice-captain and pose a few questions or scenarios to clarify this perspective.

1. If John Terry was the captain, did that mean he was a superior player to Frank Lampard who was the vice-captain?

   No. In fact Terry and Lampard played completely different positions on the same team. Terry was a defender, and Lampard was a midfielder. Lampard was an exceptional player in his own right. He was also well respected by his teammates and ready to lead when his team needed him.

   Now if I were to apply that same logic to the marriage relationship, is a husband superior in his role in the family? No. The roles of husband and wife are two different positions on the same team. The roles of husband and wife or mother and father are very different roles with strengths inherent in each role. Just like Lampard might not have been a very good defender, I would make a pretty lousy wife. For the team to be successful I need to lead and play my position and respect and understand my wife's position.

2. Who sets the tone and direction for the team?

   Ultimately in the case of the 2012 Chelsea team that would have been the coach Roberto Di Matteo. John Terry's job as captain would have been to lead the team under the structure of Di Matteo's coaching.

That is the same role for us men as captains of our team (our families). We are under the structure of God and His game plan. We lead our families by living out the tone and direction that God would have us to do. If John Terry was leading in a way that was contrary to his coach's plan, then there would have been some issues to where he could have possibly lost his position as team captain. As husbands God has called us to lead our families, but we need to be doing it His way not ours if we want to have success as a team.

3. If there is team conflict, who is responsible for getting things back on track?

    The team captain. The team captain would most likely meet with the vice-captain to gather his or her perspective and to discuss a plan of action to deal with the issues at hand, however at the end of the day the team captain would address the conflict and be accountable to the coach if there was unrest on the team. The coach would go to the captain, not the vice-captain.

    In the role of being the captain of our teams, we are accountable to God for how we lead our families. There will be times when the decisions we make may not be popular with the vice-captain or the rest of team (our children), but it may be the decision that needs to be made to get the team back on track. Also as captains we need to take responsibility for any unrest that is in our families. My dad relayed a point to Jaime and I when we were engaged to be married that has always stuck with me. He said "Since the fall when sin entered the world, man has always been trying to run from responsibility and woman from submission." As captains, the buck needs to stop with us. As men we need to take responsibility for the state of our team, not blame it on someone else.

4. What happens if there is discord in the captain/vice-captain relationship?

    I have no idea if Terry and Lampard got along as players, but I am sure if there was discord between them in their roles that it would affect the whole team. If Lampard tried to undermine Terry's leadership whenever he could or try to take over his position as captain, then there would most definitely be unrest on the team. The psychological, emotional, mental and relational aspects of the team would all be jeopardized. Anyone who has coached a team where this happens knows how hard it is to rectify and get the ship going in the right direction again.

Working out discord in our marriages needs to be a priority for our teams to run as God needs them to. There is going to be trial in that relationship. In fact the devil will work overtime attacking that relationship, maybe more than anything else in your life to make sure it is unsuccessful. He realizes that if he can destroy that relationship, the whole team (family) will go down.

5. What happens if the captain loses focus on his team?

The team looks to the captain for leadership on the field, and the captain looks to the coach. The coach is not on the field with the players, but the captain is. He is right there with his teammates during the game guiding them and encouraging them. It happens in sports that sometimes he will get injured or have an off day, and the vice-captain is there to assist him.

Our focus as captains of our teams needs to first be our relationship with the Coach (God) and second the relationship with our vice-captain (wife). Getting those priorities straight allows the team (our families) to operate successfully. If as men we aren't regularly connected to God to get His wisdom and guidance to lead our families, we will lose our focus. This will happen at times, and our wives often step up into that captain role as Lampard did for Terry. However, it is our job to get back into the role the Coach has for us and lead as He needs us to do.

As men we need to understand that loving and honoring our wives well teaches our sons how to properly treat a woman and our daughters how they should be treated by a man. Walking this out has the potential to not only change the atmosphere of our own families but the world around us. The devil knows this and sends his best players after your team. Keep in mind from Chapter 5 when we discussed that opponents have to plan how they will stop good players. They don't have to worry about players who aren't any good at the game. If you're living in sin and not leading your family, the devil will probably leave you alone. You're an ineffective leader and player, and your team will not have success.

So reading on in Ephesians Chapter 5 it informs us as husbands how we are to love and lead. It says "Husbands, love your wives, just as Christ loved the church and gave himself up for her (Ephesians 5:25

New International Version). Jesus gave up His life for the church. He gave up his life for you and me. As Christians we are to follow Christ's example in this. In Luke 9:23 (New King James Version) Jesus pulls his disciples together and tells them "If anyone desires to come after Me, let him deny himself, and take up his cross daily, and follow Me." So following Christ's example we are to deny our flesh and live daily for our wives and children. This is how God wants us as men to love our families. This is how we lead and live a life that is worthy of submission.

God also calls us to honor our wives. In 1 Peter 3:7 (New Living Translation) it says "In the same way, you husbands must give honor to your wives. Treat your wife with understanding as you live together. She may be weaker than you are, but she is your equal partner in God's gift of new life. Treat her as you should so your prayers will not be hindered." The word "weaker" in this verse is referring to physical strength, nothing else. I understand that some women are stronger than men physically, but on average it's true that men are stronger. Also God's view is not one of superiority and inferiority in the marriage relationship as it states "she is your equal partner."

So if loving my wife is giving my life for her, what does honoring her look like?

Let's think about that answer in terms of your favorite team that you played on. How did you feel about those teammates you went to battle with day in and day out, every practice and every game? The sweat, blood and tears that you shared and endured together. How did you see those guys? How did you talk about those guys? Did you honor them with your thoughts, words and actions? How did you feel when another team tried to disrespect one of those guys? Do you feel the same way about your wife? Do you honor her in the same way?

If we go a bit further with this example, how would your teammates feel if they found out you were spending time with another team? If you were practicing with that team. If you were thinking about joining that team. Do you think they'd be upset or feel betrayed? Do you think they would question where your loyalties lie? Of course they would. They would feel dishonored. The same goes for us as men when our eyes and thoughts wander towards other women. That could be in the form of pornography or a coworker we find attractive or someone else's wife. It could go as far as having an extramarital affair or having an emotional affair (one where you seek this person for relationship and support instead of your spouse) or having multiple affairs in your mind through images and fantasies online. The world tells us "There's no harm in looking. That's not cheating," however Jesus took a different view on this in Matthew 5:28 (English Standard Version) when he says "But I say to you that everyone who looks at a woman with lustful intent has already committed adultery with her in his heart."

Honestly the "You can look, but you can't touch" lesson we were taught as kids never worked out very well. We could never really help ourselves but to touch what we were looking at. Jesus tells us that if we look with lust in our heart, we've already sinned. He is trying to put up a big danger sign for us. Affairs and betrayal and dishonoring don't just come out of nowhere. They start with the eyes and move to the mind and then move to action.

Jesus warns us about this in Matthew 6:22-23a (New King James Version) when he says "The lamp of the body is the eye. If therefore your eye is good, your whole body will be full of light. But if your eye is bad, your whole body will be full of darkness." It's no wonder the devil wants us to think that there is no harm in looking. Corrupting the eye can corrupt the whole system.

I am not throwing any stones at anyone when it comes to this topic. I have struggled with sexual sin from my youth as I talked about earlier in this book. Many Christian men I have talked to do as well. I thought getting married would take it away, but that didn't happen either. God wants us to enjoy a healthy sexual relationship with our wives, and in it we honor Him and our wives. In Proverbs 5:18-19 (New International Version) it says "May our fountain be blessed, and may you rejoice in the wife of your youth. A loving doe, a graceful deer- may her breasts satisfy you always, may you ever be intoxicated with her love."

So if it is God's plan and design for us to enjoy a healthy sexual relationship within the context of marriage, then what gets in the way? If we think about it should it be any surprise that the devil will try and attack that marriage relationship in any way he can? Should we be surprised that he will do whatever he can for us as men to look for gratification outside of marriage? Probably not. We need to understand our adversary and his game plan against us.

Job knew the importance of what he allowed himself to see when he wrote in Job 31:1 (New International Version) that "I made a covenant with my eyes not to look lustfully at a young woman." He knew the consequences of what he did with his eyes. I read a book many years ago that has helped me quite a bit in this area called *Every Man's Battle* by Stephen Arterburn and Fred Stoeker. There is a lot of really practical and helpful advice to help in our battle against lust in this book, however two concepts that I found to be quite beneficial are "Bouncing Your Eyes" and "Starving Your Eyes." Simply stated bouncing your eyes is "training your eyes to bounce away from sensual sights in the women and images around you." We have built synaptic pathways in our brains that have caused us to bounce our eyes *towards* the sensual things around us, not away (Arterburn & Stoeker, 2020, p. 117). Starving your eyes is a process that requires "starving out all sexual gratification delivered through the eyes except that which involves your wife (Arterburn & Stoeker, 2020, p. 131)."

This process seemed crazy, albeit impossible, the first time I read it, however those concepts began a change in me. They began to renew my mind. They started the process of rewiring those synaptic pathways. Honestly when I was deep in my sexual sin I felt helpless to stop it. I felt I couldn't change if I wanted to. I had no idea the destruction I was inviting upon myself through my eyes. It is very similar to the reward system activation in our brains that occurs with drug-seeking behavior for drug addicts. That is what I was doing with all of the sensual images I would seek out with my eyes. I needed to make a break from that pattern in order to get better.

What's in Your Water Bottle?

When I speak with my patients about the times they feel overwhelmed or go into a panic, I have them visualize a water bottle. I talk to them about how each stress is adding a little more water into that bottle until it is overflowing. When it overflows that is when we are out of control and want more than anything to put the water back in the bottle. Unfortunately that is impossible, since the bottle is already full. The mind is reacting to this and making some space for you through that anxiety attack. The mental and emotional work in this is often preventative in nature. We have to be aware of how we are feeling. How am I right now? How full is my "water bottle?" We need to employ positive coping skills and behaviors in our lives to make room *in our bottles* for the inevitable struggles that come each day.

That is how I felt when it came to sexual sin. My "water bottle" was so full with all of the images and sensual things around me that I paid attention to that I felt helpless. I was at a tipping point all the time, and I didn't realize I was the one filling the bottle. I needed to come to an understanding that these images weren't just pornography. These images and sensual things were on TV, billboards, movies, social media, female coworkers, etc. In essence they were everywhere.

In Chapter 2 we looked at James 1:13-15 where it talks about temptation leading to desire, and desire leading to sin. Bouncing my eyes became my way of not letting temptation lead to desire. If I noticed my flesh wanting to look at some image or someone I would simply look away. I would not allow the temptation to become desire. I would turn off the TV. I would put down the phone. I would turn my gaze the other way when driving down the highway. The actions of bouncing and starving my eyes started to give me space in my "water bottle" and began to give me back control over my flesh. I was stopping the reward activation from the *drug-seeking behavior*. I began to be able to focus my eyes and sexual energy on "the wife of my youth." Now don't get me wrong I still struggle with sexual sin and need to repent at times, but things are much better than they used to be. I try to be consistently aware of what I allow my eyes to see which has helped me immensely in the area of sexual sin and honoring my wife with my mind and body.

When I am tempted and fall into lustful thoughts I pray and refocus myself by remembering who is on my team and who is not on my team. Hint: the person we are having sinful thoughts about is not on our team. She is someone else's daughter, wife, sister or aunt. More importantly she is God's daughter. She is made in His image. I need to treat her with respect in light of that truth. We also need to remember what it says in 2 Peter 2:19b (New Living Translation), "For you are a slave to whatever controls you." I need to remind myself of this truth and fight against the control of the flesh. Keep in mind that the transforming and renewal of our minds (Romans 12:2) takes work, just like it took work to transform and renew our bodies as athletes.

Honoring with Our Words

There will never be a marriage where there isn't conflict and arguing from time to time; same goes for probably any team that you played on. I would actually argue that it makes for a healthier marriage to be able to emote and communicate how we're feeling with one another. We just need to do it respectfully.

What words do we speak about or to our spouse? How do we speak about them to our friends? What do we say about them in public or at a party?

We all know that a team that trash talks itself and its teammates is going to struggle to play together on the field, and it is the same thing for us in our marriages. In Luke 6:45 (New King James Version) it says "A good man out of the treasure of his heart brings forth good; and an evil man out of the evil treasure of his heart brings forth evil. For out of the abundance of the heart his mouth speaks."

We will speak with our mouth the thoughts we harbor in our heart. If I have mean, hurtful and disrespectful thoughts towards my wife, then that is what will come out when the heat gets turned up in life. And we all know the heat gets turned up from time to time. This is why it is important to fill our hearts daily with God's words. Our teams (our families) are watching and listening to us all the time. What I say to my vice-captain matters. Remember that the power of life and death is in the tongue (Proverbs 18:21), so let's make sure we are speaking life. The adversary wants to divide us and our teams. Let's not give him that foothold in our thoughts and words.

It's Not Hopeless

Some of you reading this may be saying to yourselves that things are too far gone in my marriage to save it. It doesn't matter what I do, say or think at this point. I felt the same way at one point as I wrote about it in Chapter 6. Remember when things feel hopeless, God is able. He is rooting for you. We are reminded of this from the life of Abraham. In Romans 4:17-18 (The Message) it says:

> We call Abraham "father" not because he got God's attention by living like a saint, but because God made something out of Abraham when he was a nobody. Isn't that what we've always read in Scripture, God saying to Abraham, "I set you up as a father of many peoples"? Abraham was first named "father" and then became a father because he dared to trust God to do what only God could do: raise the dead to life, with a word make something out of nothing. When everything was hopeless, Abraham believed anyway, deciding to live not on the basis of what he saw he couldn't do but on what God said he would do.

If you're in that boat in your marriage, do you dare to trust God to do what only He can do? Do you believe He can raise your dead relationship to life? Do you believe He can make something out of nothing? Will you believe anyway when everything feels hopeless? And will you decide to live not on the basis of what you can't do but on what God said He would do? My marriage is a testimony to that word 22 years later. Don't lose hope. Draw near to God, and He promises to draw near to you (James 4:8).

Training Your Team

For the remainder of the chapter we are going to focus on our influence on the rest of our team, our children. Growing up in Christian circles we are told that the roles of a husband and father are ones of being a provider and a protector. If I keep my family safe and provide a roof over their heads, clothes on their back and food on the table, then I have done my job. This is all true, and Paul speaks about how if we don't do these things we have denied the faith (1 Timothy 5:8), however I see a third job we as fathers have and that is to prepare our team (Provide, Protect and Prepare). We do this by training our children to be able to effectively handle the road of life ahead of them.

As I write this book I am in the middle of my journey of parenthood, well at least the middle of it where my kids are living under my roof. None of us are perfect in the parenting game. My kids have definitely voiced how much they don't like me on multiple occasions throughout my journey thus far. If I were being honest the words "I hate you dad" have been thrown around a time or two. Those times are never fun for any of us as parents, however the advice I give my patients who come in for family therapy is that your job is not to be your child's friend, it is to be your child's parent. Furthermore specifically for me, it is to be my children's dad. My kids will have many friends throughout their lives, but they will only have one father. It is important to not forget that. I have met with many parents who have been so worried about their children liking them and wanting to be friends with their kids that their children no longer respect them. That desire to be liked caused them to forfeit that place of authority in their children's lives.

Being a team captain and a good team captain means that you hold a standard of expectation for the rest of the team. You need to live that out as an example to the rest of the team, but in holding that standard you will have players on your team that won't like you from time to time. All of the best team captains throughout sports knew when to call out the team when it was necessary to get the best results.

I grew up in the 1980s and witnessed the back and forth battles between the Boston Celtics and the Los Angeles Lakers during that decade. During the 1984 NBA Finals between those two teams the

Lakers beat the Celtics by 33 points in Game 3. After the game the captain of the Boston Celtics, Larry Bird, was interviewed and called his team out saying that they "played liked sissies" and didn't play with heart. The captain said what needed to be said, and the team responded. The Celtics would go on to win the next two games and eventually the NBA Championship that year as they beat the Lakers in game 7.

As a father this does not mean that you are to be abusive or demeaning to your children or to be calling them "sissies," however it does mean we are to lead and push at times to get our children to grow up. We need to speak the truth in love (Ephesians 4:15) to them. Sometimes our idea of love in this regard is off base. Often we view love as being calm and kind and tender which it is, but that is only one side of the coin. Imagine if one of your children starts walking out into traffic on a busy street corner. Is it loving for us to say in our sweetest and softest voice "Be careful honey, you could get hurt?" Or is it loving in that circumstance for us to yell as loud as we can "Hey get out of the street!" before that child gets hit by a car? The answer seems pretty clear.

God gives us some boundaries in this process when he says "Fathers do not provoke your children, lest they become discouraged (Colossians 3:21 English Standard Version)." Also in Ephesians 6:4 (New American Standard Bible) it says "Fathers, do not provoke your children to anger, but bring them up in the discipline and instruction of the Lord." Our words need to have purpose behind them, and that purpose is to raise our children "in the discipline and instruction of the Lord." Larry Bird's words were harsh, but they had purpose behind them. He needed his team to play better.

In Proverbs 22:6 (King James Version) it says "Train up a child in the way he should go: and when he is old, he will not depart from it." As athletes we all understood what it meant to train. There was a purpose to the training. We were working our bodies and minds to become game ready. The verses above instruct us to do the same with our parenting.

If God commands us to train our children and bring them up in the discipline and instruction of the Lord, how do we do that if we don't know what His instructions are? How do we train our children in God's playbook if we don't know it ourselves? This is where we need to start. I can't lead a team and follow through on God's game plan if I don't know it. I need to learn it, study it and live it out.

Knowing Your Team

In order to effectively train your team you need to know your team. If you expect to have influence on your teammates and for them to listen to you, then you need to spend time with them. Your position of authority within the team structure will only go so far. A captain's example to the team in terms of work ethic and dedication is important, but to get the most out of your teammates takes relationship, and relationships are built through time and availability. Your team needs to trust you and your leadership. They won't truly follow you otherwise.

God impressed a boundary upon me as a young parent to help me in this endeavor. I still try to stick to it today but with a lot less success if I were being honest. He told me to put my cell phone away when I got home from work. I would put it in a drawer and not check emails or surf the internet or return calls or whatever until the kids were in bed. It would force me to be focused and just spend time with them. I wanted my kids to know that I was physically and mentally with them. Sometimes I would be back in my boys' room exhausted from my day at work and fall asleep on their floor, and my oldest son would still thank me for hanging out with them. It impressed upon me that it wasn't some magic formula of quality time that my children needed. They just needed me to be present.

It's also important to understand that each one of our kids are unique. One of my wife's uncles favorite lines when it came to his kids (a boy and two girls) was "I've got three kids, one of each." It always made us laugh, and when we had three of our own we began to understand what he meant. Each one of our kids are very different and are gifted in different ways.

Something I talk to my clients in family therapy about is the mistake of doing a "one size fits all" parenting method. Some of the disciplinary and relational techniques that work for one of your kids will not work for another. We all have different personalities, and so do our children. As a coach this was also clear to me when I realized that each of my players responded differently to different coaching styles. I still kept my team standard as discussed in Chapter 4, so all of the players would be on the same page. However I needed to tailor my approach to the individual players in order to get the most out of them. The same is true for us as fathers. We need to have rules and expectations in our homes or what I like to call "non-negotiables" when I am doing family therapy, but our parenting approach to our individual children needs to fit their personalities in order to be the most effective.

So how do we better understand those personalities? Well how did you get to know your spouse and what they liked and didn't like? You spent time with them. You made mental notes of what worked and didn't work. If you took her out on a date to a certain restaurant, and she didn't like the food, then you didn't keep going there on subsequent dates. We can't keep doing the same things with our kids if they aren't working. On top of that there are many different personality tests and inventories available to help us better understand ourselves and others. They can shed valuable insight into our preferences and provide better ways to communicate. A family therapist could also be very beneficial in this regard.

In sports when a game is not going as planned, a coach needs to make some changes at halftime to get the team going in the right direction. Adjustments need to be made. Sometimes those times of crisis and argument in parenting are when we need to call a time out and regroup. My wife and father-in-law got into a big fight when she was in high school. I didn't know her back then, but from what she told me things got pretty ugly. I imagine all parties involved lost their tempers and some words were exchanged that either side wished they could've taken back. My father-in-law did something though in the aftermath of this that changed the trajectory of their relationship to this day. He had the wherewithal to see that he and his daughter weren't connecting. There may have been disobedience and defiance, but he saw that the relationship needed help. They started meeting for coffee weekly in the morning. It became a time to push pause and get to know one another again which had a profound effect on them both and allowed my father-in-law the space to effectively speak into his daughter's life.

Don't be afraid to push pause and try something new. Remember that your children come from you but are also different from you. God has a distinct purpose for you and your life and a distinct purpose for each of their lives. We are not to live our lives vicariously through them. Our job is to love them and train them to grow into their purpose.

Take Them to Practice

Another important aspect of being the captain of your team is that we need to take our team to practice. The practice field for this training is the church. The church is the place where we are studying God's playbook, where we are practicing fellowship, worship and service to others. A good church should be a place where we are equipped (Ephesians 4:11-13) to go out into the world to love and serve others. It is not just another social club.

What does your church do for the community? How is it engaging the issues in the community and the world to make them better?

The church is the practice field, not the game field. The world outside the four walls of the church is the game field: your work, your school, your community, your neighborhood, your family, etc. Those are the places where we are to live out what we have practiced in the church.

I remember pulling one of my teams together after they lost a game in which I knew they didn't play as well as they could have. I told them "We don't practice as hard as we do, so that we can have a good scrimmage against each other at the end of practice. We practice hard, so we can be ready to play our best at game time." The church is meant to be the same thing. It is a place for us and our children to practice, so we can be ready to minister to the world around us.

Jaime and I spent many years volunteering in our local church doing the prayer teams, running a small group, working in the nursery, helping to facilitate a health and wellness group and volunteering at various events. These were all ways we practiced as God was preparing us to engage others for Him in our community.

From here we stepped out on to the game field. An example of this was when our oldest son was going into elementary school, and we got an email telling us the different academic scores of the schools in the district. The school our son was going to scored pretty low, and we had the option to send him to a better performing school. I was of the mindset to send him to the better school, but Jaime said we need to pray about it and have faith for our local school. So we prayed.

God then led her to go and meet with the principal, and Jaime asked if it was okay to go to the flag pole at the front of the school and pray for the state of the school. The principal gave her permission, and she started praying there once a week. She tried to gather some of her friends, and some of them came. Jaime would also go from car to car in the drop off line at school on that prayer day and invite others to join her. Sometimes people came, and some days she prayed on her own. This act of faith didn't come without some resistance and ridicule from others at times, but remember no one steps out on to the game field thinking they won't take a few hits.

She then got involved in the PTA (Parent Teacher Association) for that elementary school. For the next eight years Jaime worked as a treasurer, vice-president and president to change the culture of that school in the way that she and the other parents could. All three of my kids as well as many other children thrived at that *lower performing* school. In fact Jaime got word one day that one of the parents of the highest performing elementary school in the district heard about one of the events she was facilitating and made the statement "How come we aren't doing that? I thought we were the distinguished school."

We live in a town in Southern California where we actually get snow due to its elevation. With the snow we get a deluge of people who come through our area to sled and play in the winter conditions they don't get where they live. Unfortunately with those people comes an ungodly amount of trash. Another "game field" experience for us in our community came from trying to address this issue. When discussing the concern with the local authorities it seemed as if everyone would pass the responsibility to another organization. Jaime began to meet with the heads of these local authorities individually (trash service, forest service, police and chamber of commerce) and gathered them all in a town meeting to come up with a plan. Along with that every Sunday afternoon during the winter months she would coordinate a time for community members to pick up trash around town. Sometimes many people would show up, and sometimes it would just be our family. Our kids were never happy about it, but it taught them how to serve.

Fight through Resistance

If the church is the practice field, then wouldn't it make sense that the devil would want to keep us and our families away at all costs. Jesus addresses this in The Parable of the Sower in Matthew 13:22 (New Living Translation) when he says "The seed that fell among the thorns represents those who hear God's word, but all too quickly the message is crowded out by the worries of this life and the lure of wealth, so no fruit is produced." As Christian men we have heard God's word, but we have to fight against it being "crowded out" if we want fruit to be produced. I'm sure all of us as husbands and fathers want a fruitful and Godly life for ourselves and our families. There is always going to be something, some worry of life or lure of wealth that gets in the way (work, sports teams, trips, etc.). I understand that a lot of us have jobs on weekends and things come up. Churches are also cognizant of this and offer many service times throughout the week and online services.

Imagine if you will the following scenario which hopefully will drive the point home. As a father if one of your teenage kids who was on their high school varsity team came to you and said "I don't want to go to practice today. I'm tired from staying up late last night playing video games with my friends." What would you say? It's not too big of a stretch for me to think that all of us would respond by telling our child that he or she made a commitment and needs to go to practice. We would do this to teach them discipline, to stick to their word and to follow through.

If we would do this for our kids with sports, making sure they get to practice, when easily the vast majority of them will never become professional athletes, then why would we not do this when it comes to getting them to the "practice field" of church to fill them with the things of God which will benefit and enrich them for the rest of their lives? In 1 Timothy 4:8 (Holman Christian Standard Bible) it says "for the training of the body has a limited benefit, but godliness is beneficial in every way, since it holds the promise for the present life and also for the life to come."

We also need to remember that more things are caught than taught. What that means is we model to our children the behavior and values we want to see. We have to live it out. We can talk at them all day long, but they will *catch* those things we do, not what we say.

I understand making this happen can be quite difficult. I've heard it all with my own family. "Sunday morning is the only day I get to sleep in." "None of my friends will be there." "Why do we have to go every week?" "I hate church; it's so boring." We need to remember that the devil is never going to make it easy for us when it comes to going after the things of God. He wants us and our families to be the unfruitful seeds that fall among the thorns (Matthew 13:22). I had a pastor once who told his kids when they were growing up "If you want to live in my house, sleep in my beds and eat my food, then you're going to church." There wasn't room for negotiation. Joshua made the famous declaration to Israel in Joshua 24:15 (New Living Translation) when he said "But as for me and my family, we will serve the LORD."

Note that Joshua's wife didn't make this proclamation. Joshua did. Too often it seems the spiritual direction and guidance of the household is left up to the mothers and grandmothers. I'm not saying that is in any way as a knock against them, and I am glad that someone in the home is standing in the gap for the things of God, but it does come with a consequence. There was an article written by Robbie Low for Touchstone Magazine called "The Truth About Men and Church" which outlined a survey that was administered in Switzerland in 1994 and stressed the incredible importance of fathers and churchgoing. The following is an excerpt from the article:

> "In short, if a father does not go to church, no matter how faithful his wife's devotions, only one child in 50 will become a regular worshipper. If a father does go regularly, regardless of the practice of the mother, between two-thirds and three-quarters of their children will become churchgoers (regular and irregular). If a father goes but irregularly to church, regardless of his wife's devotion, between a half and two-thirds of their offspring will find themselves coming to church regularly or occasionally (Low, 2003)."

Let those numbers sink in and begin to understand your influence as men in terms of the spiritual life of your children. We only have a short time in which our children are under our roof. We need to make that time count.

In Judges 2:6-10 (The Message) it states:

> After Joshua had dismissed them, the People of Israel went off to claim their allotted territories and take possession of the land. The people worshipped God throughout the lifetime of Joshua and the time of the leaders who survived him, leaders who had been in on all of God's great work that he had done for Israel. Then Joshua son of Nun, the servant of God, died. He was 110 years old. They buried him in his allotted inheritance at Timnath Heres in the hills of Ephraim north of Mount Gaash.

> Eventually that entire generation died and was buried. Then another generation grew up that didn't know anything of God or the work he had done for Israel.

Why did this other generation that grew up not know anything of God or what He had done?

It seems to me that this generation stopped speaking about the things of God. They didn't raise their kids to know Him and His love for them. As you read on in Judges 2 the people of Israel abandon God and chase after other gods, and it says in Judges 2:15 that "They were in a bad way." None of us want that for our families, but it's up to us just like it was with the generation after Joshua to lead our families and decide who we will serve.

In closing out this chapter, we need to take ownership and step up in leadership of our marriages and children. The hard truth in this is that our marriages and families are a reflection of our leadership as husbands and fathers. If we don't like how things are going in our homes, we need to take a look in the mirror. Most great teams in sports history reflected the leadership of their captains as well. Those team captains set the tone for how the team played and how they treated one another. Often their leadership was the difference between mediocrity and greatness.

Chapter 11

How to Be a Father to the Fatherless

"A coach will impact more people in one year than the average person will in an entire lifetime."

-Billy Graham

It says in James 1:27 (King James Version) that "Pure and undefiled religion before God and the Father is this, to visit the fatherless and widows in their affliction, and to keep himself unspotted from the world." The same verse in The Message version says "Anyone who sets himself up as 'religious' by talking a good game is self-deceived. This kind of religion is hot air and only hot air. Real religion, the kind that passes muster before God the Father, is this: Reach out to the homeless and loveless in their plight, and guard against corruption from the godless world." Anyone who has been around the church or has heard or read the Bible has probably heard something to the effect that "God wants us to be a father to the fatherless." I always found myself scratching my head on that one.

How do you do that? What does that mean for me? Adopt a bunch of kids? How do you visit widows in their affliction?

Honestly when I read that verse it seems pretty in your face as well. If we say we are "religious" or that we follow God but are not reaching out to the fatherless and widows we are "self-deceived" and full of "hot air."

This made me take a pause and ask God what he wanted from me in this regard. Between working a full-time job and having a private practice on the side, being married and raising three kids I wasn't really sure how I could fit more in to my day. Was this one of those things I could put on the back burner and say I would have to do in a different season of life when I wasn't so busy? Maybe, but I kept getting a check in my spirit about it. God wanted me to do more than just take care of my own family, and He wanted me to get going on that now in my life. He did not want me to neglect my family or my marriage, but God wanted my impact for His kingdom and loving others to be more than just my family. He wanted my witness of His love to "shine like lights in a dark world, and you offer them the teaching that gives life (Philippians 2:15-16 Easy-to-Read Version)."

Loving and leading my family is my first priority, but they are not the ones in the "dark world." They are not the fatherless ones. This does not mean I take care of someone else's children to the neglect of my own. I am still commanded to "bring them up in the training and instruction of the Lord (Ephesians 6:4 New International Version)." I've heard a lot of stories in my profession where children have been turned off to the things of God because their parents' *ministry* took priority over their own families.

So how do we do both? How do we "visit the fatherless and widows in their affliction" while still loving and taking care of our own families? God will open our eyes and give us opportunities if we ask Him. Here is how He did it with me.

Coaching Kids

All of my children have been involved in youth sports. I believe in the values and lessons that sports teaches them. Once our kids started playing soccer and basketball and track it became pretty clear to my wife and me that these organizations needed help with coaching and referees and such. A good rule of thumb when looking for opportunities to love and serve others for God in the community around you is to go where the need is. One year we received an email from the regional commissioner for our local soccer league that he needed three Under 10 age group coaches for boys' teams. That's 30 eight and nine year old boys in our little town that wouldn't be able to play that season, because there wasn't anyone to coach them.

Looking at the typical practice and game schedule for a youth soccer team there are usually two practices a week and a game on Saturday. As a parent, if you have a child on a team, you will most likely have to drive your child to those practices and games and wait by the field until the practice or game is over and then head home. You are already spending the time there in your hectic life and schedule.

I asked myself "What if I took the time I was already spending in getting my children to and from practices and games and volunteered to coach?" I initially had the thought that I didn't want to get involved but decided it was worth the extra effort. From that point forward I have been coaching one or two of my children's teams every year.

So how about you?

I already know the excuses running through your head. I don't have time. I don't know how to play. I'm not good with kids. I'm not good with people. I'm not athletic enough. So let's step back and look at the specific email I received in the preceding paragraph. We were talking about coaching soccer for eight and nine year old boys. You do not need to be Ronaldo or Messi to coach soccer for eight and nine year old kids. You just need to show up. There are administrators and trainers within those organizations that can help you to learn. I have been coaching for many years now and God has used that experience to allow me to love my family and also be a father to the fatherless.

Don't get me wrong coaching can be hard and can be a stretch on your family system at times, especially the older and more competitive the teams become. Also everyone will have an opinion (players and parents alike) about what you should be doing, who you should be playing, why you're winning or not winning, that you're pushing the players too hard in practice or not pushing hard enough. Most of those people who want to put their two cents in have never coached before and aren't interested in helping you. I have learned over the years to block that stuff out. I am respectful to everyone and listen but have realized I can't take those things to heart.

Furthermore if you know me I may seem mild-mannered at times, but I am of Viking ancestry and was raised in Philadelphia, so when it comes to sports and coaching I yell a lot. I expect a lot out of my players and push them when I don't feel I am getting their 100% in practices and games. I don't verbally degrade anyone, but I can get loud. My wife used to cringe a bit when I coached and would do check-ins with the parents. I would also get emails from the administration on a weekly basis to tone things down. I would try, but that is not how I am wired. I am telling you all of this to show you that I am not perfect. I'm human. I have my strengths and my flaws, but over the years I have stuck it out.

In the World, Not of the World

We have all seen the bumper stickers about being "in the world but not of the world." Jesus talks about this when he is praying for his disciples in John 17:14-16 (New King James Version). In verse 15 He says "I do not pray that You should take them out of the world, but that You should keep them from the evil one." This concept has gotten skewed over the years to be a situation for some Christians in which they have really limited their interactions with anyone who believes differently than they do. They may invite their neighbor to church on Christmas or Easter, and when their neighbor politely declines they say to themselves that they did their part. I asked, and they turned me down. Being in the world and loving our neighbors needs to be so much more than that. There is a good book out there called *The Art of Neighboring* by Jay Pathak and Dave Runyon which outlines some great practical ways to obey Jesus' command to love our neighbors from Mark 12:31.

It's been my experience from simply asking people or putting a flyer on their front door inviting them to church has not been a very effective way to reach people for Jesus. When Jesus gave his disciples the Great Commission in Matthew 28:19-20, His first instruction was for them to go. The second command was to make disciples. We need to go first before we can make disciples. We can't expect people to come to us on our terms.

For the remainder of this chapter I want to outline the ways God has used my life through coaching kids as a ministry tool to "go" and reach my community and allow me to be a father to the fatherless and visit widows in their affliction. Before I get into that though I want to preface this by saying that if you do decide to coach you will need to do it with the principle of this book found in Deuteronomy 6:5, doing it with all your heart, soul and strength. You will never reach and influence others if you are unorganized, have a bad attitude and are mean to people. As discussed in Chapter 6 regarding the qualities of a good player, you will need to strive for excellence in order to have an effective voice. The quality that you bring to the field as a coach will give you the platform to speak into the lives of these kids and parents. It won't work otherwise.

I didn't have some magic coaching formula when I started. My goal was simple. I wanted each player to be better than they were at the beginning of the season. I figured even if they were in better physical shape that would be something, but I also wanted them to progress with their skills and knowledge of the game. As a team I focused on how they treated each other and worked together. Obviously also the hope was that we would win a few games along the way. Actually that isn't really true. I wanted to win every game.

Built In Prayer List

At the beginning of each season I was given a list of my players and their parents' names. Right there I had a built in prayer list for the next few months. I'm not going to lie and say that I prayed for those people every day, but I would say a quick prayer for each player and his family on my commute from work to practice twice a week. The player list would also give me some insight into their home life, specifically if there was divorce or a single parent home simply by the names of the parents delineated with different last names and addresses. As I got to know my players and their stories throughout the season I would be able to pray more specifically about their health, academics and home life.

Also before every game I would bring my team together on the field and after we discussed the positions and plan for that game, I would pray for the team and for their opponent. When I first started doing this I was nervous that there would be some complaints from parents, but that never happened. I figured for a lot of those kids that was the only time all week or maybe in their lives that they heard someone pray. One of the neat things I got to witness was some of the players that I had coached for some years began to volunteer to pray for the team before our games. I'd also get a reminder from a number of them if I got distracted trying to get ready for a game and forgot to pray.

Developing Competence in the Fatherless

God wants us as men to be an influence upon those children who don't have a father. We are commanded to minister to the fatherless. Do the fatherless need a mother? Does James 1:27 say we are to visit the motherless? The answer to these questions is pretty clear. So this verse is actually a charge to men. You might say to yourself "That doesn't apply to me. That book of the Bible was written some 2000 years ago." Funny you should bring that up if you are under the impression that the father situation is getting better as time has gone by. There is actually a federal government program which has been around for a while that is specifically aimed at the lack of fatherly influence in our society. The following is taken from their website, aptly named www.fatherhood.gov in their "About Us" section:

> The Claims Resolution Act of 2010 (CRA) reauthorized funding for the National Responsible Fatherhood Clearinghouse (NRFC). The NRFC was initially funded through the Deficit Reduction Act (2005) for the "development, promotion, and distribution of a media campaign to encourage the appropriate involvement of parents in the life of any child and specifically the issue of responsible fatherhood, and the development of a national clearinghouse to assist States and communities in efforts to promote and support marriage and responsible fatherhood (National Responsible Fatherhood Clearinghouse, n.d.)."

If the problem is getting better since the book of James was written I'm not sure why the federal government is now pouring resources into men becoming better fathers. Note how the words "responsible fatherhood" is written twice in excerpt above. Recall how we discussed that since the fall in the Garden of Eden men have been running from responsibility, so this is nothing new. We all know and so does the government that the father situation isn't getting better, and that the repercussions are felt throughout society.

So why is the role of fathers so important?

In my Human Sexuality course in graduate school, my professor Dr. Bruce Stokes, talked about the importance of the role of the father as a parent. Dr. Stokes said that a father fulfills the male need for competence and the female need for safety and trust. An absent or withdrawn father leaves a son with a sense of incompetence, and an absent or withdrawn father leaves a daughter with a sense of undesirability. To further explain this he told a story about a little boy who drew a picture, and his mom praised him for it and put it up on the refrigerator. When his dad got home from work he said "What is that ugly looking scribble on the fridge supposed to be?" The boy's feelings were hurt, and the dad apologized, however the boy learned over time that dad was going to give it to him straight. He wasn't going to sugarcoat things (B.H. Stokes, personal communication, May 11, 2004). I know this is a generalization, but for those who have boys or work with boys this should resonate.

Could it be that many of our issues in society today come from men who have a lack of competence that comes from absent or withdrawn fathers?

There are not many other positions in life where a man has that type of influence to build competence in a group of young men, fatherless or not, than as a coach. As a coach I hold all of my players to the same standards. They do the same amount of sprints and push-ups. They are all required to finish distance runs under the same timeframe. They all do the same drills. Many of my players complain about it and tell me they can't do it. I tell them that they are capable, but they're afraid to push themselves and afraid of the pain they will face to accomplish that goal. I don't change my level of competence for my players. I have them keep trying until they reach the goal. It is amazing to see the faces of those boys when they finally can accomplish the goals set before them. I try to teach them that the only way you gain self-confidence is to set a goal for yourself that you don't think you can reach, and then accomplish it.

This dynamic is captured extremely well in a scene from the movie *Remember the Titans* (2000). The movie is based on a true story of two high schools in 1971 in Virginia, one black school and one white school. The schools were given a federal mandate to integrate, and the football coach of the black school (Herman Boone) is appointed as the head coach. The former coach of that school (Bill Yoast) becomes his assistant. The following is an excerpt from the script in which the two coaches are discussing a situation in which Coach Yoast pulls one of the players aside to console him after Coach Boone confronted that player (Petey) in front of the team.

Boone: Listen about Petey.

Yoast: No thanks required Coach.

Boone: Thanks! You challenged my authority in front of the entire football team Coach! Now you think you're doing these boys a favor taking them aside every time I come down on them, protecting them from big bad Boone. You cutting my legs from under me.

Yoast: Some of the boys just don't respond well to public criticism. I tell them what they need to know, but I don't humiliate them in front of the team.

Boone: Which boys you talking about? Which ones you talking about? I come down on Bertier. I don't see you coddling him. Come down on Sunshine. I don't see you grab his hand and take him off to the side. Which boys you talking about? Now I may be a mean cuss, but I'm the same mean cuss with everybody on that football field. The world don't give a damn about how sensitive these kids are, especially the young black kids. You ain't doing these kids a favor by patronizing them. You're crippling them. You're crippling them for life (Bruckheimer & Oman, 2000, 55:22).

The movie follows that high school team and their path to winning the Virginia high school state title that year. The example from the excerpt above depicts a coach who was willing to hold a standard of competence for all of his players. His players rose to that standard and finished that season with an undefeated record, ranked as the second best team in the country.

As a coach in youth sports you will have an opportunity to teach boys and young men to be competent at something and to push themselves to do something they didn't think they could do. That is a gift they will have for the rest of their life.

Visiting Widows and Orphans in Their Affliction

Some years back I had a boy on my team whose dad tragically died in a car accident. I also had a boy whose mom was dying of cancer. We have a neighbor who has played on my daughter's team whose dad died. To this day that neighbor girl comes over most days of the week after school, plays with my daughter and eats dinner at our house. I jokingly call her "my other daughter." We all sit down together at the table, pray for dinner, talk about our days and most of the time she even helps out doing the dishes with my kids. I also pick up the boy and his younger brother, who lost their dad in a car accident, every week and take them to our local Christian Service Brigade meetings and church youth group meetings. Christian Service Brigade is an organization designed to help boys grow into Godly men with a heart for serving others (www.csbministries.org). Through these relationships that have grown out of my time as their coach I have been able to speak into their lives and lead them to a relationship with Jesus.

The "widows" of this day and age are our single moms. A number of my players over the years came from fatherless homes. As a coach I was able to build a relationship with many of them and speak some fatherly advice into their lives. I would spend time on the phone outside of practice talking with these single moms and their sons about a range of topics from academics to how they were treating their siblings to smoking and drug abuse. The respect that was built on the practice field allowed me to visit "widows in their affliction." A lot of those moms would tell me that their son listened to me, and they so appreciated the calls. I also made sure at the end of each season that the players and parents knew they could reach out to me if they needed anything.

Presenting the Gospel

At the end of every season there would be a team party in which ribbons or trophies were handed out. I would address the team as a whole and each kid individually talking to them about aspects of their game and sportsmanship they improved on throughout the season and things to work on for next year. This was also an opportunity for me to share some of my story and testimony and how that has affected my philosophy of life. A few years back I had some bracelets made that said "All On The Field" on one side and "DT 6:5" on the other. The "DT 6:5" was short for Deuteronomy 6:5, a verse that's been referenced throughout this book. My talk to the teams would be about giving their all in life. It wasn't about being perfect but getting back up and trying again and knowing that God is there to help them to give their best. I would talk to the players and families and invite them to come visit with me afterwards if they wanted to know more about a relationship with God and how He is there to help them. Over a couple of seasons a number of the players had memorized the verse and some gave their hearts and lives to Jesus as well.

Preston Brown

     Preston Brown grew up in Camden, NJ. He is one of six kids who were all raised by a single mom. In an interview he talked about his childhood saying "At the time I started playing football, we were borrowing electricity from the neighbor's house with an extension cord. We couldn't use our front door because there were guys dealing on the front steps. We had to go around back. I didn't even see that as a rough situation. It was just life." Brown got an opportunity to play football in the neighboring Pennsauken Youth Athletic Association by lying and using someone else's address.

     He noticed his life was different when he got to play in Pennsauken. He recalled "Every one of those black kids I played with on that team, they had a mom and dad. They lived in a house. None of us in Camden had dads that lived at home with us. It was mom, grandmom, aunts. There were no male figures. It was amazing to me that we could be living blocks away and have completely different lives."

     Eventually his secret got out and the head coach Rob Davis confronted him. Instead of kicking him off the team though the coach told him that he also lived in Camden. Coach Davis told Brown to be on a certain corner every day at 5:15 for practice, and he would pick him up. For the next two years Brown was on that corner at 5:15.

     That team went on to win a championship and Brown was recruited by a number of private high schools, however he decided to play football for his high school team, Woodrow Wilson High School. He had a successful career, becoming salutatorian, lettering in football for 3 straight years and receiving 31 football and academic scholarships to schools including Stanford and Notre Dame. Brown chose to attend Tulane University. He played well enough in college to get tryouts from the Buffalo Bills and New York Jets but didn't make either team. Brown did however play professionally in the Arena Football League.

     He got married, started a family and went back to school and earned his Master's Degree. Brown was the proverbial success story of a kid who made it out, however he didn't stay away. In 2015 he moved his family back to Camden and took the head football coaching job for his alma mater. In 2012 the team had a winless season, but within three seasons with Brown at the helm he turned the program into a championship winning team. Many of his players have gotten college scholarships and chances of their own to rewrite their stories.

     In concluding the interview Brown said "People like me, and the people I grew up with in my community, we were taught it was us against the world. People knew Camden as a negative place, and I always wanted to change that narrative. The young people we send out into the world, to these colleges, to become great and productive citizens- they are the ones who change it (Morgan, 2021)." Brown grew up without a dad but became a father to the fatherless and changed the narrative for so many young men and the entire community around him.

This is the power of coaching. This is the power of developing competence in young men. This is the power of being a father to the fatherless.

Chapter 12

<u>How to Join the Team</u>

"The child, in danger of the fire, just clings to the fireman, and trusts to him alone. She raises no question about the strength of his limbs to carry her, or the zeal of his heart to rescue her; but she clings. The heat is terrible, the smoke is blinding, but she clings; and her deliverer quickly bears her to safety. In the same childlike confidence cling to Jesus, who can and will bear you out of danger from the flames of sin."

-Charles Spurgeon

Some of you may have been reading this book, and there has been a tugging in your heart and your spirit. You've been doing this battle alone, and you're tired. Or you know you haven't been living up to your potential. Or you know that some things are off in your life, but you feel helpless to change them. God, like our coaches in the past, want to help us through these things and succeed in this life, however I need to ask myself "Am I on His team?" It's pretty clear we can't get coaching and guidance from a coach if we never joined the team. I'm going to share a story from my past that may help you in this decision process.

It was a summer day, and I was home on break from college. I grew up in Pennsylvania playing in the state's creeks and rivers ever since I can remember. We didn't have a pool, so that's what you did to cool off. You put on your "river shoes," which were just old sneakers and went swimming. One Saturday my brothers Dave and Dan and I drove to one of the creeks in the area that had a dam built across its width. You could jump from one end of the dam from about 20 feet up into the current, and we spent the afternoon taking turns making the jump.

As the day wore on my brother Dave told me that you could actually walk underneath the dam across the width of the creek. He told me that he and some of his friends had done it. The dam was built at a 45 degree slope, and you could run down it and jump off the end into the water and push your way up under the dam. I'm guessing it would be somewhat similar to getting behind a waterfall. From there you could walk the width of the creek underneath the dam. At least that's how the story went. Here's how our story went.

Like many boys of that age using our mid-brain and being a bit impulsive, we decided we needed to give it a try. Dave volunteered to go first since he had done it before, and I was going to watch how he did it. He proceeded to run down the dam and jumped off into the water. I didn't see him for a decent amount of time, so I thought he must've gotten under the dam. Just then I saw his head pop up out of the water for an instant and then get pulled back under the water. About 10 seconds later his head popped up again and again he went back under. The next time his head popped up he yelled to me for help.

It's interesting when I think back on this story, because at that moment I did not hesitate at all. As soon as I heard my brother calling for help I ran down the dam and jumped in the water. I didn't consider that it might be dangerous for me too. I just knew that my brother needed me. When I got in the water I realized that the water at the bottom of the dam was probably about seven or eight feet deep, because I remember hitting the bottom with my feet but I couldn't stand on the bottom without my head being under the water. I grabbed Dave and pushed him downstream which freed him from the undertow current that was happening. I remember watching him float downstream feeling a sense of relief, only to be pulled under the water a second later. I was now caught in that current.

It's strange what runs through your head at a time like that. I remembered when I was a kid, and my grandfather had built a house on the banks of the Delaware River. We would spend our summers as a family there, and that's where I learned to swim as a child. One day while I was swimming my legs got caught in some weeds at the bottom of the river, and I couldn't free myself. My body was underwater, and I recall looking up at the sunlight shining through the surface of the water wishing I could swim up. I'm sure I was frantically splashing with my hands, and I was definitely stuck and panicking. Next thing I remember is seeing a pair of hands break the surface of the water and pull me out. It was my mom. She carried me to the bank of the river and wrapped me in a towel. I coughed and spit out water but was okay. That memory flashed through my mind as my body was being spun around like I was in a washing machine. I also visualized a newspaper headline in my head of my death from drowning and thought about what my parents would be feeling, not enjoyable thoughts for sure. I fought my way back to the surface and caught another breath before being yanked back under the water again.

Time seemed to slow down, and I began to think "How am I going to get out of this? There has to be a way out." At that point I prayed. Guessing I should have done that first, but it was a crisis and that didn't seem to be the first thing that came to my mind. It was a quick prayer for help. The answer then dawned on me as I remembered a lesson I learned while I was involved in a kayaking club in college. I had done my fair share of canoeing in the past and had learned some things about rivers and currents, but it was the instructor for that club who told me about these kinds of currents. I fought for another breath as my body was getting more tired and tried to remember what he had said to do. The lightbulb went on, and I recalled him saying that this kind of current circulates under the surface of the water, so each time you try to come up it pulls you under. However if you swim to the bottom of the river you'll get under the circulating current, and it'll push you free.

To this day I honestly can't remember if that is the advice he told me or if God was whispering that to my spirit. In any case it definitely goes against your instinct to go deeper under the water to get out, but I didn't have too many choices at that point. I told myself I would fight my way to the surface for one more breath and then swim as hard as I could for the bottom of the creek. Staying where I was wasn't an option. Eventually I would tire out and drown, so I went for it. I got to the surface and took as deep of a breath as I could and swam for the bottom. I felt my body being pulled along the bottom of the creek by the current as I swam and was able to come up to the surface for air about 20 or 30 feet downstream.

Dave was waiting for me there. Our eyes met as I took a big breath. All I can remember saying to him is "Are you good?" He responded, "Yeah I'm good." I replied "Okay. You wanna go home?" His response was "Yeah, let's go home." We were pretty quiet and shaken up as we swam across the current back to the bank of the creek. We yelled for our brother Dan and told him we were leaving. At the time of the writing of this book, Dave is the Executive Director of a camping ministry in Pennsylvania, and he uses that story as a way to share the gospel with his campers and how we were rescued.

And that is Jesus. That is the gospel. That is how He loves us.

He wouldn't hesitate to run down the dam and jump into the current and push us free. In fact that is what He did when He died for our sins on the cross. I think too often we don't realize we are stuck in a circulating current in life being spun around and around and fighting for each breath. I had an atheist friend of mine ask me once what makes Christianity any different from any other religion. My simple answer was Jesus. He is the only deity in any religion that came down to our level to save and rescue us. All the others require us to ascend towards them.

Jesus gets in the currents of life with us and rescues us. He cleans us up and asks "Are you good? You wanna go home? Let's go home."

We join His team by acknowledging Jesus as our Lord and Savior (rescuer). We confess (say we're sorry) our sins (where we fall short and have messed up) and follow Him (give Him our ALL). That's it. That's how you join His team. There are no try-outs or standards we have to meet. We can come as we are. It's not about the words or what you can do. It's about your heart. It's about a decision you make to call out for help and surrender your life to Him and His plan for you. There is nothing you can do to earn it. It's a gift.

If you need some words to help you, here is a simple prayer:

"Jesus, I need you to rescue me. I can't do it on my own. Thank you for dying for my sins and paying the price for all of the wrongs I have done. I ask for your forgiveness. I want to be on your team and give you my all. Amen."

For those of you who prayed that prayer, you have joined the best team you will ever play on. Don't forget that getting on the team is just the start, and a good coach pushes you to reach your potential. In order to be that better player you need to practice. You need to get out on the field. Find a church where they study the "playbook" and where you can get around a team that will help you and encourage you to be the best you can be.

Closing Thoughts

The 400-meter dash is a race that is a bit misleading in its name. It falls into the category of a sprint, but those of us who have ever competed in this race might tell you otherwise. It is hard, and it hurts. Racers line up in their assigned lane and use starting blocks just like any other sprint. When the starting gun fires you sprint like any other sprint, but the distance of the 400 affects your body in a different way than the 100-meter or 200-meter dash. Carson Boddicker, in his article "How to Train for the 400-Meter Dash" wrote:

> The 400-meter dash is a challenging event that requires an athlete to possess both a high level of speed and specific conditioning. The 400-meter race requires contributions largely from the anaerobic glycolytic system, which produces large amounts of metabolic waste products that ultimately lead to the "burning" feeling in your legs and reduced ability to produce more energy as the race moves on further. Therefore, you must train to facilitate your body's use and removal of these products to ensure that you are able to run faster and longer (Boddicker, n.d.).

That "burning" feeling in my legs would kick in somewhere between 200 to 300 meters into the race. All of a sudden my muscles would begin to feel weak and rubbery. I would feel like I was fighting against my own body to keep going and maintain the pace necessary to finish and win. In that last third of the race my legs would continue to weaken as I was unable to get enough oxygen. However as I would make that last turn into the final 100-meter straight away my mind would slow down, and my vision would focus on the finish line. I knew it would be over soon, and something in me allowed me to dig down and push through. Most times when I crossed the finish line I would jog it out for 10 or 20-meters to slow down and then would end up falling over in the infield completely spent. Many times I would have to throw up as well. Every time I really ran that race my body would have nothing left at the end. That race took everything I had, and to run it well I had to give it everything I had.

As stated above from the article "The 400-meter dash is a challenging event that requires an athlete to possess both a high level of speed and specific conditioning." In order to push through that spot in the race where your legs start to fail, you need specific conditioning. It matters how you train. Conditioning matters. The right combination of distances and intervals and plyometric exercises prepare your body to be "able to run faster and longer." Without the right conditioning you won't be able to compete, and you won't finish strong.

Many times in the race of life I am running now I get that "burning feeling" and a "reduced ability to produce more energy as the race moves on further." I have to understand and take seriously that how I train (physically, mentally, spiritually, emotionally, socially) today provides me with the "specific conditioning" I need to live well and finish well. What I do matters. My commitments matter. Keeping my focus matters. Seeking God and His wisdom first in life to inform my decisions and direction matters. Studying and memorizing His *playbook* and how He wants me to live matters. Taking care of myself consistently matters. How I speak to and love my wife matters. How I love and lead my children matters. How I show up and work each day matters. How I treat my friends and neighbors matters. How I volunteer and take care of my community matters. How I steward my wealth and finances matters. How I love and serve God and others matters.

There are No Shortcuts

There is a sobering section of scripture that speaks to our choices and what we do with the days we've been given. In 1 Corinthians 3:12-15 (New Living Translation) it says "Anyone who builds on that foundation may use a variety of materials- gold, silver, jewels, wood, hay, or straw. But on the judgment day, fire will reveal what kind of work each builder has done. The fire will show if a person's work has any value. If the work survives, that builder will receive a reward. But if the work is burned up, the builder will suffer great loss. The builder will be saved, but like someone barely escaping through a wall of flames." The choices and "work" of my life will be tested to "reveal what kind of work each builder has done." There are no shortcuts. We all reap what we sow (Galatians 6:7). We get out what we put in.

If a runner doesn't properly train, he or she will not be able to effectively compete. Paul writes in 1 Corinthians 9:24-26 (New International Version) "Do you not know that in a race all the runners run, but only one gets the prize? Run in such a way as to get the prize. Everyone who competes in the games goes into strict training. They do it to get a crown that will not last, but we do it to get a crown that will last forever. Therefore I do not run like someone running aimlessly; I do not fight like a boxer beating the air." God wants us to *run* in this life "in such a way as to get the prize." He wants us to live with purpose and intention, not "like someone running aimlessly." He wants our life and work to have value. God doesn't just leave us out on our own to figure all this out. He wants to coach us. He wants to teach, rebuke, correct and train us (2 Timothy 3:16), so that we can live life to the fullest (John 10:10). He wants to be with us, to help us and strengthen us (Isaiah 41:10). God wants to be that coach running down the sideline alongside us instructing us and cheering us on as we go.

To this day I still think about some of those 400-meter races from time to time. To be honest I enjoyed the shorter sprints a lot more when I competed, but the 400-meter dash is the race that connects with me in my life today. The 400-meter dash is how I think God wants me to run this life. I will face battles and days and seasons that feel like I'm at the 250-meter mark of the race with my legs "burning." He wants to train me to be ready for those times. As I make the turn into the final 100 meters God wants me to stay focused on the finish, not turning to my right or left (Joshua 1:7) and give everything I have (Deuteronomy 6:5). He wants me to leave it all on the field. And when I cross that finish line, if I ran my race well, then I can echo the words of 2 Timothy 4:7 (New Living Translation) where it says "I have fought the good fight, I have finished the race, and I have remained faithful."

I want to humbly thank you for taking the time to read these words, these thoughts and these stories. It is my prayer that they have been encouraging and have filled you with hope for the days ahead. I know it feels at times that we live in a day and age where it is almost impossible to know what is real and true. We are fed information and misinformation all the time, and it's hard to know what to expect and how to fight the battles in front of us. Know that God is the same yesterday, today and forever (Hebrews 13:8). His game plan is trustworthy, and He will equip us with everything we need to finish our race.

References

Chapter 2

Taylor, B. (2018, March 9). What Breaking the 4-Minute Mile Taught Us About the Limits of Conventional Thinking. Retrieved from https://hbr.org/2018/03/what-breaking-the-4-minute-mile-taught-us-about-the-limits-of-conventional-thinking

Chapter 4

McCash, S. (2008). Morning rounds: Daily devotional stories (Donna R. Hadley, Ed.). Loma Linda University Press.

Jurgen Klopp explains how he cultivates his incredible relationship with players. (2020, March 19). Thisisansfield. https://www.thisisanfield.com/2020/03/jurgen-klopp-explains-how-he-cultivates-his-incredible-relationship-with-players/

Chapter 5

Whitt, C. (2013, September 27). *Shooting Hoops with Twenty One Pilots*. Retrieved from https://www.altpress.com/aptv_video/shooting_hoops_with_twenty_one_pilots/

Mckay, B., & McKay, K. (2016, July 19). The Herschel Walker Workout. Retrieved from https://www.artofmanliness.com/articles/the-herschel-walker-workout/

Spink, K. (1997). *Mother Teresa: A Complete Authorized Biograpy*. Harper Collins. New York.

Chelsea defender Antonio Rudiger reveals the tactical difference between Thomas Tuchel and Frank Lampard. (2021, February 14). Metro. https://metro.co.uk/2021/02/14/chelsea-news-antonio-rudiger-reveals-difference-between-thomas-tuchel-frank-lampard-14081573/

Chapter 6

Paulson, J., & Bazemore, S. (2010). Prenatal and Postpartum Depression in Fathers and Its Association with Maternal Depression. *Journal of American Medical Association, 303(19)*, 1961.

Chapter 7

Chronic Disease in America. (2019, October 23). Retrieved from https://www.cdc.gov/chronicdisease/resources/infographic/chronic-diseases.htm

Pizzo, A. & DeHaven, C. (Producers) & Anspaugh, D. (Director). (1986). *Hoosiers* [Motion Picture]. United States: Orion Pictures.

Bradberry, T. (n.d.). How Complaining Rewires Your Brain for Negativity. Retrieved June 1, 2020 from https://www.talentsmart.com/articles/How-Complaining-Rewires-Your-Brain-for-Negativity-2147446676-p-1.html

Bandelow, B., & Michaelis, S. (2015). Epidemiology of anxiety disorders in the 21st century. *Dialogues in Clinical Neuroscience*, 17(3), 327.

Newman, T. (2018, September 5). Anxiety in the West: Is it on the rise? Retrieved from https://www.medicalnewstoday.com/articles/322877

Greenberger, D., & Padesky, C. (1995). Mind Over Mood: Change How You Feel by Changing the Way You Think. New York, NY: The Guilford Press.

Steber, C. (2018, May 3). 11 Ways Your Brain Changes When You Don't Treat Anxiety. Retrieved from https://www.bustle.com/p/11-ways-your-brain-changes-when-you-dont-treat-your-anxiety-8907435

Chapter 9

Peyton Manning biography. (2020, May 26). Retrieved from https://www.biography.com/athlete/peyton-manning

Check, D. (Producer) & Waksman, G. (Director). (2010). *30 for 30: Four days in October* [Motion Picture]. United States: ESPN/MLB Productions.

Chapter 10

Benjamin, D. (n.d.). How to become a team captain. Retrieved September 10, 2020 from https://www.breakthroughbasketball.com/players/how-to-be-a-team-leader.html

Arterburn, S. & Stoeker, F. (2020). *Every man's battle: Winning the war on sexual temptation one victory at time* [E-book]. Colorado Springs, CO: Waterbrook.

Low, R. (2003, June). The Truth About Men & Church. Retrieved from http://www.touchstonemag.com/archives/article.php?id=16-05-024-v

Chapter 11

National Responsible Fatherhood Clearinghouse. (n.d.) Retrieved February 5, 2020 from https://www.fatherhood.gov/about-us

Bruckheimer, J. & Oman, C. (Producers) & Yakin, B. (Director). (2000). *Remember the Titans* [Motion Picture]. United States: Walt Disney Pictures.

Morgan, K. (2021, June). Preston Brown: The Comeback Coach. Retrieved from https://sjmagazine.net/people/preston-brown-comeback-coach

Closing Thoughts

Boddicker, C. (n.d.). *How to train for the 400-meter dash.* Livestrong. https://www.livestrong.com/article/192482-how-to-train-for-the-400-meter-dash/

Made in the USA
Columbia, SC
11 March 2024